Michael Hollings & Etta Gullick

as was his custom

PRAYERS AND READINGS
FOR EACH DAY OF THE YEAR

MAYHEW-McCRIMMON

Great Wakering

First published in Great Britain in 1979 by
MAYHEW-McCRIMMON LTD
Great Wakering, Essex, England

ISBN 0 85597 287 5

Edited by Robert B. Kelly and Ann O'Brien
Cover and lay-out by John Honeyands
Printed by Mayhew-McCrimmon Printers Ltd

Contents

Introduction

WHY and HOW

The purpose of this book is prayerful.

During the 1970's we have produced a series of books of prayers of differing shapes and sizes and feeling. These received an overwhelming welcome, and it is safe to say that since then there has been a veritable avalanche of books of prayers.

To add another cost us serious thought and took a long time to germinate. The balance tilted in favour of doing this book for two reasons. There has been a constant flow of requests for yet another book from the Hollings-Gullick team. To this was added the remarks of booksellers that a through-the-year book of prayers was a frequent demand from customers in the shops.

The pattern is simply a day by day offering of a prayer of passage of writing. The choice of authors, their historical age and the style of their writing is very varied. A multitude of other selections could have been made, but our attempt is to carry through the message of the month, according to the season of the year, both in the Church's calendar and our own pattern of winter, spring, summer and autumn.

In order to use the book properly and to gain the most value personally or in a group, we suggest that a Bible is essential. We set out deliberately to make the bible a daily companion, knit in with the feast day, the meditative prayer or reading, and the theme of the month.

It is not our intention to try to lay down exactly how anyone should use the book. There must be hundreds of ways. But it is of the essence of prayer as we know it personally that there is very great variety, even when a person is well advanced in the spiritual life. We should urge that no one slavishly follows each day, or each reading, or feels bound to meditate. Take it as it comes; come to it as you are.

There will be times when no word is necessary, except perhaps the word of the heart expressing knowledge of being loved and loving. But there will also be times when dryness, blankness and lethargy seem to dominate all we are, and then someone else's thought can help us through the desert. Only use what is useful. The more direct our contact with God, the deeper and more word-less our relationship, the purer and truer will be the union with the one who is the Word but is beyond all words.

For anyone who feels utterly unskilled, why not try some simple pattern like the following. Again, discard it as soon as you have grown out of it. The Lord is interested in your growing, not in your use of systems or techniques.

* Sit, stand or kneel quietly in your room, in church in the garden or countryside . . . indeed anywhere.
* Let stillness enter you, quieting yourself with a word of love or praise or thanks.
* Ask God to send his Spirit into your heart.
* Take nourishment from the prayer or reading.
* Pause to let the thought sink into your whole consciousness.
* Respond with silence or a single word.
* If time permits and you feel it would be good, move on to the Scripture reading, and let this, too, sink in. Alternatively, leave that till another time.
* At the end of your period of prayer-time, it is some-times good to use the Lord's Prayer. It is also a happy thought to praise the Lord and thank him.
* Throughout the day, it is to be hoped that the thought from the prayer and reading will surface in quiet moments. It may be necessary and useful to recall the thought deliberately until the pattern has become a routine.
* Try to make a habit throughout the day of referring all happenings, thoughts, etc., to the Lord. This is a gradual process which will build a closeness of his presence, and will engage many of the events which

would otherwise re-appear in prayer-time as distractions.

We hope that what we have put together may be of value to you in your growing relationship with God. We hope, too, that you will remember us in your prayers.

Feast of All Saints   Michael Hollings
1 November, 1978   Etta Gullick

December

Waiting and preparing
Sharing
Witness

The Church begins her new year about the beginning of December, with the commencement of Advent.

The Advent season is a strange mixture of thinking about the end of time, the second coming of Christ, and all the while looking forward in preparation for our joyous celebration of the birth of Jesus at Bethlehem.

In a way, this combination sets us off for the year by implying that the whole of existence is telescoped. Hundreds and thousands of years have passed in creation and in God's plan of salvation. When we look at it all in terms of years it is too big to cope with. If we reduce the creation-fall-house-of-Israel-incarnation-death-resurrection and early history of Christianity all within a year, the precise form becomes more manageable, if more superficial.

The purpose of our month before Christmas and few days immediately following the celebration is to give us a breathing space in which individually or together we can let this wonderful expression of God's love for us sink in.

Often, the sheer busy-ness of the pre-Christmas rush in the world of today threatens to extinguish the expectancy and the spiritual deepening of our preparation. If we can take time each day to ponder a prayer and a reading we shall be more ready to share the joy of Christmas with God and each other. Of course there will be earthly preparations too. Just simply do not let them engulf all your time and energy. It is Jesus' birthday. Make a present of yourself to him.

In the passages we have chosen there is diversity moving from the second coming through preparation to the actual commemoration of

Jesus' birth. In the calendar of the Church the birthday is followed by the birth into the 'joy of the Lord' of some saints and witnesses to Jesus, his life and his power.

Absorb something day by day and you need have no fear.

Beginning the year with praise

Praise him, praise him,
praise him in the morning,
praise him in the noontime.
Praise him, praise him,
praise him when the sun goes down.

Love him, love him,
love him in the morning,
love him in the noontime.
Love him, love him,
love him when the sun goes down.

Anonymous.

Reading: Ps 8 How great is your name, O Lord our God.

You must wake up now

It is hard for us to believe that you will really come again. We, your people, have been waiting so long that we have forgotten how to watch and pray.

We are so busy with our own concerns that we do not think about your second coming.

We have lost our sense of awe and have made the remembrance of your first coming cosy and respectable.

We cannot believe that judgment will fall on us; it does not seem possible.

Give us sense of expectancy;
Teach us to be watchful and to pray when we watch;
Show us how to read the signs of the time;
There are so many disasters, wars, revolutions,
earthquakes, fires, that we become indifferent to them.
We forget that they happen to people like us who feel and suffer,
And that they could happen to us at any time.
Is this the judgment you foretold, events which happen to individuals?
And is your second coming something which happens in our hearts,

if we are ready and watchful?
O help us to stay alert, watching and praying, full of hope and
      expectancy!

Reading: Mk 13:32-36 You never know when the time will come.

DECEMBER 3
The feast of St. Peter Damian

The craftsman beats gold with his hammer to get rid of the dross. He
assiduously scrapes away with his file so that the vein of glittering metal
may gleam more brightly. 'Just as the potter's jar is tried in the furnace so
are just men tried by temptation.' That is why Saint James says, 'Count it
all joy, my brethren, when you meet various trials.' They who suffer here
and now on account of their evil deeds rightly rejoice when there is an
eternal reward for their good deeds laid up for them.

Peter Damian (1007-1072)
from a *Letter*

Reading: 2 Cor 4:7-18 Earthenware jars.

DECEMBER 4
The gift of hope

Give me hope; but before I can come to live in hope I need to learn to trust
you more. It is not easy to live happily in today's world without the
courage and support which you give. Life without faith surely must
always have been difficult at any time in the history of mankind. Now
when society is changing so rapidly and the world as we know it is
collapsing, is must be terrifying to live without you. With modern
weapons piling up and becoming more world shattering, judgment may
be closer than we think, therefore Lord, give us, give me, the gift of hope.
To trust in you I need to love you more, so increase my love so that my
hope and trust may grow stronger.

Reading: 1 Pet 1:13-21 Faith and hope in God.

DECEMBER 5
Hoping against hope

Someone has said that to say 'all shall be well, all manner of things shall
be well' is just the expression of an easy optimism. Is this so Lord? I
always hope all will come right in the end because all things are in your
hands, but life does not seem to work out this way for all. You predicted
war, famine, earthquakes, floods, the lot, but in the end you would come
again, and then for those who love and serve you, all would be well. Lord,

help me to understand and to realize that there must be suffering, pain and striving before we see you come again, but give us hope, too, that in the end, all will be well.

Reading: Is 25:6-9 Our God in whom we hoped.

The feast of St. Nicholas — 'Santa Claus'

Thank you for Saint Nicholas; after so many centuries we still commemorate his kindness to young people by the giving of presents to children at Christmas. Help us to respect the innocence of children and to remember that your Son told us to become single-minded like them in our pursuit of you. You give to us love, joy, peace and so many other wonderful gifts; teach us to share with others your goodness not only by the giving of presents to children and friends, but by the offering of ourselves and our time to those who come to us in need. We ask this through Jesus Christ, your Son, whom you sent to us on the first Christmas day.

Reading: 2 Cor 8:1-9 About giving and the generosity of God.

He is coming

He is coming, he who is present in every place and fills all things, that in you he may bring the salvation of all men. He is coming, who came to call not the righteous but sinners to repentance, that he may recall those wandering in sin. Therefore, do not be afraid. God is in the midst of you; you will not be moved.

St. Andrew of Crete (*c.* 660-740)

Reading: Rom 8:31-39 Who can be against us?

The feast of the Immaculate Conception of Mary

As we prepare for Christmas, we can spend time looking at your plan, Lord God Almighty. We watch you sending a messenger to a young woman called Mary. You entrust her with the life of your Son, who is to be the Holy One — God with us. We marvel at your trust placed in her. We thank you for choosing Mary, and so giving us her example of beautifully open acceptance of your will in her life. Help us as we watch and wait to form in our hearts the will to answer 'YES' in our lives to anything you ask of us. Make us generous and loving, Lord.

Reading: Lk 1:26-38 Announcing the conception of Christ.

DECEMBER 9

The power of the Bible

Thank you, Lord for the Bible: for its ability to give us each day new vision and new power; for its capacity to reach to the roots of our inner life and to refresh them; for its power to enter into the innermost structures of mind and spirit and fashion them anew. For the Bible, and its power to beget faith and sustain it, we give you, thanks and praise; through Jesus Christ our Saviour.

Dick Williams
from *Prayers for Today's Church* (1972)

Reading: Rev 21:1-7 A new heaven and a new earth.

DECEMBER 10

The Bible discloses the riches of God

Lord, who can grasp all the wealth of just one of your words? What we understand is much less than what we leave behind, like thirsty people who drink from a fountain. For your word, Lord, has many shades of meaning just as those who study it have many different points of view. The Lord has coloured his words with many hues so that each person who studies it can see in it what he loves. He has hidden many treasures in his word so that each of us is enriched as we meditate on it.

St. Ephraim (*c.* 306-373)
from *On the Diatessaron*

Reading: Rom 11:33-36 How rich are the depths of God.

DECEMBER 11

Thy Word of Life

Grant me, O Lord, to take the Book of books
as from the hands of thine angel,
With expectancy of faith,
With brimming hope, and
With the love that kindles knowledge;
to open and re-open, read and re-read,
ponder and re-ponder, mark, learn and
inwardly digest -
    THY WORD OF LIFE
Convey to me, O Holy Spirit,
through the familiar phrases, fresh understanding;
through passages passed over or unapprehended, new treasure;

14

through thy grace, — insight, conviction, guidance, revelation, glory.

Eric Milner-White (1884-1963)
from *My God, My Glory*

Reading: Rom 15:4-13 To teach us something about hope.

The feast of St. Jane Frances de Chantal

We are always wanting this and that, and although we have our sweet Jesus resting on our heart we are not satisfied; and yet this is all we can possibly need and desire. One thing alone is necessary — to be near him. You know that at the birth of our Lord the shepherds heard the divine songs of heavenly beings; this is what scripture tells us. But nowhere does it say that our lady and Saint Joseph, who were closest to the child heard the angels' voices or saw the marvellous radiance; on the contrary, they heard the child crying, and by the wretched light of some poor lantern they saw the eyes of this divine boy full of tears and saw him chilled by the cold. Now tell me would you not rather have been in the dark stable which was full of the baby's crying, rather than with the shepherds ravished with heavenly music and the beauty of this marvellous light?

As Saint Peter says, it is good for us to be here . . . Love God crucified in the darkness, stay near him and say, 'It is good for me to be here.'

St. Francis de Sales (1567-1622)
from a *Letter to St. Jane de Chantal*

Reading: Ps 131 Lowliness and trust before God.

St. Lucy: Feast of light — an invitation to share

Come walk with me; come share my life;
You must know the shadows if you would know the light.
To be the body of the Lord in this world,
To have his Spirit coursing through my soul,
To know the passion of my Jesus in his love for every man,
To show his mercy in the shadows of this land.

From a folk hymn

Reading: Mt 16:24-28 If anyone will follow me.

The feast of St. John of the Cross — mystic

And O, ye lamps of fire,
In whose resplendent light
The deepest caverns where the senses meet,

15

Once steeped in darkness dire,
Blaze with new glories bright
And to the lov'd one give both light and heat!

How tender is the love
Thou wak'nest in my breast
When thou, alone and secretly, are there!
Whispering of things above,
Most glorious and most blest,
How delicate the love thou mak'st me bear!

St. John of the Cross (1542-1591)
from *Poems*

Reading: 1 Jn 4:17-19 We love God because he first loved us.

DECEMBER 15

The voice in the wilderness

I thank you for the messengers you send us who remind us that we should bear witness to you in our world today. We often want to forget their voices which seem to cry out for the truth to be known and for your gospel of love and service to be preached in a world which appears only to care for material things and for the interests of their own group. Give me courage to show that I recognise that spiritual hunger is at least as important as the material by my witness to the good news of your Son Jesus Christ.

Reading: Is 40:1-11 Prepare a way for the Lord.

DECEMBER 16

Preparing the way

John the Baptist, who came to prepare the way for the coming of your Son, preached the need for repentance to the people of his time. Show us how we should repent before we remember Christ's first coming this Christmas. We are selfish and over-concerned with worldly things. Show us how we can prepare a way for Christ to enter into our lives in a fuller way so that like John the Baptist we may decrease that he may increase; teach us the kind of lowliness which allows Jesus Christ to be born in our hearts so that our lives be more and more conformed to his.   Amen.

Reading: Mk 1:1-11 The need for repentance as preparation for Christ's coming.

DECEMBER 17

Waiting for the coming of the Lord

Keep us, O Lord, while we tarry on this earth, in a serious seeking after thee, and in an affectionate walking with thee, every day of our lives; that when thou comest, we may be found not hiding our talent, nor serving the flesh, not yet asleep with our lamp unfurnished, but waiting and longing for our Lord, our glorious God for ever and ever.

Richard Baxter (1615-1691)

Reading: Mt 25:1-13 Watch

Praying for the kingdom of God within

According to the saying of our Lord and Saviour, the kingdom of God does not come in such a way as to be seen. No one will say, 'Look, here it is!' or, 'There it is'; because the kingdom of God is within us. The word is very near us; it is on our lips and in our heart. It is clear from this that when a man prays that God's kingdom may come, he is praying as he should, for the kingdom of God which is within him, that it may rise, flourish and reach its full growth.

Origen (c. 185-254)
from *On Prayer*

Reading: Lk 18:15-17 Welcome the kingdom of God like a little child.

The longing for God

Late have I loved you, O beauty so ancient and so new; late have I loved you! For behold you were within me, and I outside; and I sought you outside and in my ugliness fell upon those lovely things that you have made. You were with me and I was not with you. I was kept from you by those things, yet had they not been in you, they would not have been at all. You called and cried to me and broke open my deafness; and you sent forth your beam and shone upon me, and chased away my blindness; you breathed fragrance upon me, and I drew in my breath and do now pant for you: I tasted you and I now hunger and thirst for you; you touched me, and I have burned for your peace.

St. Augustine (354-430)
from *The Confessions*

Reading: Ps 42 My soul longs for you, my God.

The coming of the Light

As a lantern raises its light in a dark dwelling, so truth rises within faith in a person's heart.

From the *Alphabet of Piety*

Reading: Mt 5:14-16 You are the light of the world.

DECEMBER 21

Jesus is truly God and truly man

It is of no avail to say that our Lord, the son of the Virgin Mary, was true and perfect man, if he is not believed to be man of that stock from which the Gospel tells us he came.

Matthew says: 'The book of the genealogy of Jesus Christ, the son of David, the son of Abraham'. He then follows the order of Christ's human origin and traces the line of his ancestry down to Joseph, to whom the Lord's mother was betrothed.

Luke, on the other hand, works backwards step by step and traces his succession to the first of the human race himself, to show that the first Adam and the last Adam were of the same nature . . .

If the new man, made in the likeness of sinful flesh, had not taken our old nature; if he, one in substance with the Father, had not accepted to be one in substance with the mother; if he who was alone free from sin had not united our nature to himself — then men would still have been held captive under the power of the devil. We would have been incapable of profiting by the victor's triumph if the battle had been fought outside our nature. But, by means of this marvellous sharing, the mystery of our rebirth shone out upon us. We would be reborn in newness of spirit through the same Spirit through whom Christ was conceived and born.

Consequently, the evangelist speaks of those who believe as those 'who were born, not of blood nor of the will of the flesh nor of the will of man, but of God'.

St. Leo the Great (+ 461)
from his *Letter on the Genealogy of Christ*

Reading: Mt 1:1-16 Genealogy of Jesus Christ.

DECEMBER 22

Spiritual as well as material preparation for Christmas

Dear Lord, help and strengthen me at this busy time! There is so much to do shopping for food, trying to find the right presents, preparing meals; I get so very tired and so easily irritable with family and friends. It seems such a strange way of getting ready for your Son's coming; there appears to be no time to reflect on its meaning. Help me to prepare for Christmas by finding time for quiet so that I can ponder on the wonder and simplicity of your Son's birth, and if I cannot have time alone give me inner quietness so that your peace may calm my busy mind and my preparation for Christmas may be spiritual as well as material. Keep reminding me that man cannot live by bread alone.   Amen.

Reading: Col 3:14-17 Let Christ's peace by in your heart.

The revelation of God in Jesus

God, hidden from our eyes,
Men have always been searching for you.
We probe the distances of space;
We plumb the depths of our own minds.
We find you, but never completely.
Left to ourselves we should go on searching for ever.
Only you can bring our search to its goal.

But you have done that:
You have revealed yourself to us in Jesus Christ.
As a baby he was born in a stable in Bethlehem;
As a man he died on a cross at Calvary.
In him our search has reached its goal.
God, hidden from our eyes,
Yet revealed in Jesus Christ,
We worship and adore you.

From *More Contemporary Prayers*

Reading: 1 Tim 6:11-16 Awaiting Christ's coming.

Open our hearts to increase our vision

Almighty God, Father of Light, your eternal Word leapt down from heaven, blazing out the generosity of your love in the deep silence of the night. We, your Church, are filled with wonder at your nearness to us, our nearness to you. Open our hearts to receive his life and to increase our vision with the rising dawn. In this way may our lives be filled with the glory and peace of Jesus Christ.

Reading: Wis 18:14-15 Leapt your all powerful word, or Col 1:15-20 The image of the invisible God.

The birthday of Jesus Christ

Happy birthday, Lord Jesus! I wonder how you celebrated it at home with Mary and Joseph. It was probably very ordinary and very full of family joy. Help me and all of us today, Lord, that we should join you in rejoicing and not just our selfish selves. Indeed, this was a wonderful day for your creation, an expression of your huge love that we cannot fail to see. But, all the same, help us to expand our minds and hearts so that we celebrate by giving our love — to each other, to the unlovable, to the lonely, to the deprived of this world who are your own special brothers and sisters. As you gave us the present of yourself at Christmas, so may we open the parcel of our ungenerous self-preoccupation, and feel free to give ourselves in all directions without counting the cost.   Amen.

Reading: Lk 2:1-20 Spreading the news of Jesus' birth.

DECEMBER 26

The feast of St. Stephen

Lord, you told us to love our enemies. Stephen today gives us an example of that love as he asks forgiveness for those who are condemning and killing him. Help us to follow this example and your own, Lord Jesus, by being open enough to love and forgive any enemies we have, praying for them and asking you to show them the joy of your love.   Amen.

Reading: Acts 7:55-60 Stoning of Stephen.

DECEMBER 27

The feast of St. John the evangelist

Lord, you revealed to John that 'In the beginning was the Word', that the Word was also light shining in the darkness, and the darkness could not overcome the light. On the feast of Saint John give us confidence in your power; patience to listen to you; and courage to face the darkness when it surrounds us, enlightened by trust in your love.

Reading: Jn 1:4-14 The Life, Light and Word.

DECEMBER 28

The commemoration of the Holy Innocents

Lord, this horrifying story is repeated endlessly today and for less powerful reasons. Prevent us from growing accustomed to violence, help us to defend the defenseless. Especially, Lord, give true love to parents for their children, even in the womb, that they may care for and protect them.

Reading: Mt 2:13-18 Rachel weeping for her children.

DECEMBER 29

The feast of St. Thomas of Canterbury

In Thomas, Lord, the clash of religion and politics reached a high pitch of tension. The result was bloodshed and death on the steps of the Cathedral altar. Help us to face persecution if it comes. But Lord, today we pray especially for all those who are now under pressure, in prison or deprived because of their belief in you. Strengthen them and give them fortitude in their suffering.

Reading: Mt 24:4-14 They will hand you over to be tortured.

Nearing the end of the year

Another year almost ended, Lord! I look back and my first inclination is to think about myself. Instead, I choose deliberately to look at you, to wonder at your glory, to love and thank you. You alone gave me life in this past year. You guided me, loved me this far. Thank you! As the old year dies, I ask you that I may will to die a little today and tomorrow and to myself so that I can rise again in the new year with a new life — that I may trust you, accept your love and respond with my love towards you and all you have made. Be with me through next year, Lord God of future ages.

Reading: Eccles 42:15-26 The work of the Lord is full of his glory, *or:* Lam 3:22-26 The steadfast love of the Lord never ceases.

The last day of the year

The last day of the old year has come, Lord, to be viewed by different people with different thoughts. There can be few people for whom the year has not been a patchwork. Joy meets sorrow, pain gives way to healing, happiness emerges into a desert period.

In praying on this last day, we raise our minds and hearts to you first of all in thanks . . . for being alive, for knowing your love, for seeing you pictured in your creation, for a deep sense of peace in believing.

Grant us now to go forward into next year more than ever seeking the glory of the face of Christ, radiant among our friends and neighbours and enemies too.

Grant peace in our days, grant a growing love among the nations of the world. In you will we find our peace — help us lay bare your will for us.

Reading: 2 Cor 4:1-6 The glory on the face of Christ.

The feast of the Holy Family

The home of Nazareth is the school where we begin to understand the life of Jesus — the school of the Gospel.

The first lesson we learn here is to look, to listen, meditate and penetrate the meaning — at once so deep and so mysterious — of this very simple, very humble and very beautiful manifestation of the Son of God. Perhaps we learn, even imperceptibly the lesson of imitation.

We learn the method which will permit us to understand who Christ is.

Reading: Lk 2:39-40 & 51-52 Life at Nazareth.

January

Revelation of Jesus to Gentiles and Jews
Faith and Baptism

After the birth of Jesus, the Church looks to the continuous revelation of him which comes in different ways. The early part of January is dominated by the great feast of the Epiphany, which in history has outshone Christmas. Here, the development of the revelation is in the mysterious story of the three who came from the East and afterwards disappeared again. Whatever the source and historicity of the visit, there is here a fulfilment of the prophecies of the Old Testament. Traditionally, this has always been seen as the revelation of the incarnation stretching beyond the bounds of Israel.

This light of revelation is that Jesus, the man-child, is something more. It both strengthens our knowledge of the manhood of Christ and leads us towards the further disclosure which comes through the Spirit and through John at the baptism of Jesus.

This gives us an opportunity for spending a little time in prayer about faith in our own lives — that faith which can enlighten us, but can also call for greater and fuller expression of our trust in God. We have received the Spirit ourselves in baptism, but we are often no stronger in faith than Peter was when he feared that he would drown. We need continual prayer to strengthen us, and even so things go wrong.

So we come to a period of a week during which we concentrate on the immediate and thorny problem of unity among Christians, and also the situation vis-à-vis God and the 'church' of those who do not accept Christ, whether they be Jews, Muslims, Hindus or those who claim simply to be non-believers. The churches generally impress on all who will listen that we have a duty to pray for unity.

However, there does not always seem to be much enthusiasm, and different people have different ideas as to what unity may mean. During this month there is much scope for us to grow in prayer and understanding of the necessary work for unity which we should share. We ought also to impress upon ourselves the fact that this work and prayer should not be confined to one week, but should stretch into other weeks and months throughout the year.

Consideration of the unity issue brings us to the end of the month with the realisation that there will be no lasting peace until we are truly Christian in our coming together as one, according to God's will.

Looking ahead into the New Year

For all the possibilities ahead in this new year,
    make me thankful, O Lord.
Give us wisdom, courage and discernment
    in the face of so much chaos, despair and fear.
Help us to see how, in our circumstances,
    we can contribute towards peace, faith and love.
And give us the will to translate our desires into action.

Brother John Charles, SSF
from *Contemporary Parish Prayers* (1975)

Reading: Acts 13:17-43 Paul preaches the Good News.

The human nature of Christ

What was born of Mary, according to scripture, was by nature human;
the Lord's body was a real one — real, because it was the same as ours.
This was so because Mary was our sister, since we are all descended from
Adam. This is the meaning of John's words: 'The Word became flesh', as
can be seen from a similar passage in Paul: 'Christ became a curse for us'.
The human body has been greatly enhanced through the fellowship and
union of the Word with it.

St. Athanasius (*c.* 296-373)
from a *'Letter'*

Reading: Gal 4:3-7 God sent his son, born of a woman.

The human nature of Christ

We know that the Word assumed a body from a virgin and, through a
new creation, put on our old nature. We know that he was a man, formed
from the same substance as we are. If he were not of the same nature as
ourselves, his command to imitate him as a master would be a futile one.
If he was of a different substance, why does he command me, naturally
weak as I am, to do as he did? How can he be good and just?

St. Hippolytus (+235)
from his *Refutation of Heresies*

Reading: Col 1:21-29. He has reconciled you by his death and in that mortal body.

25

The incarnation of the Son of God brings peace

The birthday of the Lord is the birthday of peace. As the Apostle says, 'He is our peace, who made us both one.' For whether we be Jews or Gentile, 'through him we both have access to the Father.'

St. Leo the Great (+461)
from a *Sermon*

Reading: Eph 2:13-18. He is the peace between us.

JANUARY 5

The star shining in our hearts

Almighty and everlasting God, who hast made known the Incarnation of thy Son by the bright shining of a star, which when the wise men beheld, they presented costly gifts and adored thy majesty; grant that the star of thy righteousness may always shine in our hearts; and that, for our treasure, we may give to thy service ourselves and all we possess; through Jesus Christ our Lord.

Gelasian Sacramentary (late 7th century)

Reading: Is 60:1-6 Everyone in Sheba will come, bringing gold and incense.

JANUARY 6

A revelation to the Gentiles

O Father everlasting, the light of faithful souls, who didst bring the nations to thy light and kings to the brightness of thy rising; fill the world with thy glory, we beseech thee, and show thyself unto all the nations; through him who is the true light and the bright and morning star, Jesus Christ, thy Son our Lord.

Gothic Missal (7th century)

Reading: Mt 2:7-12 The sight of the star filled them with delight.

JANUARY 7

Walking in the light

We praise you, O God, that the light of Christ shines amid the darkness of our world, and that the darkness has not overcome it; and we pray that his light may shine more and more into our lives, illuminating our minds with the knowledge of the truth and enabling us to walk in the way of holiness and love; through the same Jesus Christ our Lord.

Frank Colquhoun
from *Contemporary Parish Prayers* (1975)

Reading: Ps 72:1-17 or: Is 60:19-22. A universal peace till the moon is no more.

Baptism of Jesus by the Spirit

Lord, at the baptism of your Son in the river Jordan you revealed his glory to those standing by who had eyes to see, and ears to hear, and hearts to understand. At the time they may not have realized the wonder of the revelation or hardly perceived its meaning at all; it was, perhaps, only after the resurrection and coming of the Spirit into their hearts that they understood what was being revealed to them on the banks of the Jordan. You have shone your light into my heart, and I know that I must bear witness to your Son and his good news in the dark world of today. Help me to reveal you to others, and encourage me to keep on praising and thanking you for the wonderful manifestation of your glory in your Son, and for the gift of the Holy Spirit who helps us to see and to understand and to speak.

Reading: Mt 3:13-17 He saw the Spirit of God descending.

Learning from the Baptiser

Give us, O God, something of the spirit of your servant John the Baptist:
> His moral courage,
> His contentment with simplicity,
> His refusal to be fettered by the world,
> His faithfulness in witness to the end.

So may we be heralds of Christ and his kingdom and make ready his way, to the glory of his name.

Frank Colquhoun
from *Contemporary Parish Prayers* (1975)

Reading: Jn 1:19-28 The witness of John the Baptist.

Faith

Thank you, Oh Lord, for this gift of the Faith,
Jewel many-facetted. Lord let its light
Shine now all about me. I will not grasp it
To hold in my hand, bending my sight
Too closely on one single facet, for that
Might reflect my own face, not
The splendid and shining
Fierce and undying
Glory within.

John Brailsford

Reading: Rom 4:13-25 The promise of inheriting the world.

JANUARY 11

Ask for all you need

Give us, O Lord, a humble, quiet, peaceable and patient, tender and charitable mind, and in all our thoughts, words and deeds a taste of the Holy Spirit. Give us, O Lord, a lively faith, a firm hope, a fervent charity, a love of thee. Take from us all lukewarmness in meditation, dullness in prayer. Give us fervour and delight in thinking of thee and thy grace, thy tender compassion towards us. The things that we pray for, good Lord, give us grace to labour for: through Jesus Christ our Lord.

St. Thomas More (1478-1535)

Reading: Eph 6:18-19 Pray all the time.

JANUARY 12

Trusting the Lord

O God, the Father of lights
From whom cometh down every good and perfect gift;
Mercifully look upon our frailty and infirmity;
And grant us such health of body
As thou knowest to be needful for us;
That both in our bodies and souls,
We may ever more serve thee
With all our strength and might
Through Jesus Christ our Lord.

St. Augustine (354-430)

Reading: Ps 40 A song of praise and prayer for help.

JANUARY 13

Not hiding from God's face

Heavenly Father, we implore you
to send your Holy Spirit now and evermore,
that he may awaken us, enlighten us, encourage us
and enable us to advance from the comforts of our own choosing.
Turn us away from ourselves and
draw us in hope to you.
Do not let us hide from your face.
Show us your glory
and how glorious it is to cling to you.
We ask this gift for all mankind.

Karl Barth (1886-1959)
from *Deliverance to the Captives*

Reading: Acts 10:44-48 A coming of the Holy Spirit.

A prayer for mental illumination

O merciful Jesus, enlighten thou me with the brightness of thine inward light, and take away all darkness from the habitation of my heart.

Repress thou my many wandering thoughts, and break in pieces those temptations which so violently assault me.

Fight thou strongly for me, and vanquish these evil beasts, these alluring desires of the flesh, that so peace may be obtained by thy power, and that thine abundant praise may resound in a holy temple — that is in a pure conscience.

Command the winds and tempests; say unto the sea, Be still; say to the north wind, Blow not; and there shall be a great calm.

Join thou me to thyself with an inseparable band of love; for thou, even thou alone, dost satisfy him that loveth thee, and without thee all things are vain and empty.

Thomas à Kempis (1379-1471)

Reading: 2 Cor·12:7-10 My grace is enough for you.

Strengthen us

O God, our Father, we are exceedingly frail and indisposed to every virtuous and gallant undertaking. Strengthen our weakness, we beseech thee, that we may do valiantly in this spiritual war; help us against our own negligence and cowardice, and defend us from the treachery of our unfaithful hearts; for Jesus Christ's sake.

Thomas à Kempis (1379-1471)

Reading: 1 Thess 5:4-11 Let us put on faith and love.

Lord save us — we perish

O God, by thy mercy strengthen us who lie exposed to the rough storms of troubles and temptations. Help us against our own negligence and cowardice, and defend us from the treachery of our unfaithful hearts. Succour us, we beseech thee, and bring us to thy safe haven of peace and felicity.

Thomas à Kempis (1379-1471)

Reading: Mt 14:22-33 Jesus and Peter walk on the water.

The Feast of St. Anthony of Egypt

Saint Anthony did not remember the time gone by but, day after day as if he were beginning his ascetics again, he strove rather to go forward, repeating continually the words of Saint Paul: 'Forgetting what lies behind and straining forward to what lies ahead, I run straight to the goal'. He remembered also the words of Elijah: 'The Lord lives in whose presence I stand today.' He noted that in saying: *today* Elijah did not reckon the time that had passed. And so as if he was always at the beginning every day, he strove to be in the state in which he must appear before God: pure of heart and ready to obey his will and no other.

St. Athanasius (*c*. 296-373)
from his *Life of St. Anthony*

Reading: Phil 3:12-16 Keep on day by day striving to reach out to God, our goal.

JANUARY **18** **Octave of Prayer for Christian Unity**
Day 1. Praying and working for unity

In praying before you died, Lord Jesus, you prayed for all to be one as you and your Father are one. We echo this prayer today. At the same time we promise to work hard for unity according to your will. Give us faith which is strong enough to be open to the belief of others, while holding fast to truth; love strong enough to melt fear and bigotry where-ever it exists.

Reading: Jn 17:20-21 That they may all be one.

JANUARY **19** **Octave of Prayer for Christian Unity**
Day 2. The scandal of division

The division among Christians is a scandal, Lord. We admit our wrongness in not being one, and our lack of zeal at trying to cut out the cancer of disunity. How can we learn to be united in your love, so that others may see us and be attracted rather than put off? Please open our minds and hearts and wills to your Spirit who brings unity and peace.

Reading: Jn 17:22-23 That the world will realise.

JANUARY **20** **Octave of Prayer for Christian Unity**
Day 3. Seeking the way to unity

Sometimes we seem so close to being one. And then next moment, Lord, we come up against a deep underlying difference. Perhaps we do not really understand what YOU mean by unity. Perhaps we are too traditional in what we cling to, too complicated to grasp the simplicity of your truth. Unravel us, Lord God. Let us see the Way.

Reading: Jn 14:4-9 I am the Way.

Day 4. A prayer for the Jewish People

Lord Jesus, your chosen people Israel is still far from accepting you as God. What is your will for Israel? How can I help your will forward? You love the members of your people so deeply, so patiently. We Christians owe them so much, even yourself, Lord. They are still your chosen. You alone can continue to lead them forward as you did with Moses and the pillar of fire in the desert. Help us as Christians to live your love patiently, so giving an example. And listen to our prayer today that you lead and guide those of the Jewish faith ever deeper in your love and service.

Reading: Ps 89 The faithful love of God.

Day 5. A prayer for Muslims

God of Abraham, Isaac and Jacob, you are worshipped alike by Jew and Muslim. Your prophet Mohammed has preached you as the One God. He has many followers who pray and fast in strict religious zeal. We know you have your own design both for peace between people and between beliefs of different religions. By our faithful living of a Christian life, may we share in your design of worship of the one true God. To you, Lord Jesus, we leave the further revelation of yourself through the Koran and through the Gospel. Draw us closer to each other and to you.

Reading: Gen 50:1-14 The funeral of Jacob.

Day 6. Some truth in all religions

There are many religions in your world, Lord God, which are very different from Christianity. Yet, if they are in some way worshipping you, surely each has its grain of truth and goodness? Help us to come to know them personally, and allow them to know us. If they come to know our faces and our hearts and we are truly Christian, surely through us they may come to know the face and heart of your love, in your own time, Lord God of all creation.

Reading: Acts 10:34-36 The truth I have come to realise.

Day 7. Unity according to God's will

Lord Jesus, everything is in your power. You and you alone can bring us together to live in unity and peace. We do not know how or when you will bring this about. Until you do, we promise to pray and work with great zeal, patience and love for the final completion of your will. Help us to live in utter trust as you did.

Reading: Rom 8:22-25 Something we must wait for with patience.

JANUARY 25 Octave of Prayer for Christian Unity
Day 8. Feast of the Conversion of St. Paul

Lord God, on the Damascus road, you gave Paul a vision of your Son which blinded him with its glory; after his outward vision was restored you gave him an inner light and deeper knowledge of yourself through your Son, which continued to increase during his life time and was an inspiration to others. Give me a vision of your Son's glory so that like Paul I may give up everything to follow Jesus Christ and through sharing his sufferings may also experience his resurrection joy. The vision, I know, fades and the wonder is only dimly remembered, and the hard slog and the time in the desert follows as it did with Paul. Help me to keep on through adversity as Saint Paul did, and give me glimpses of glory from time to time so as to help me on my earthly pilgrimage to you.

Amen.

Reading: Acts 9:1-19 The story of Paul's conversion.

JANUARY 26
A prayer for understanding the religion of other people

There are so many countries and so many different people in the world you have made, Lord. When I am lucky enough to travel, I find men and women like myself who pray to you and believe in you. But they do not always believe what I believe I believe! I am convinced they are sincere, they want you, Lord, and so I am happy to pray with them and to believe in the width and breadth of the communion of saints where we all meet to praise and glorify your name and come to know each other. Let me learn more, Lord.

Reading: Jn 9:1-38 The man born blind.

JANUARY 27
The wonder of the world

I hope, Lord, I appreciate just a little the intricate pattern of your design for the economy of the world. As I sit down and contemplate the beauty and the mystery of so very many tiny births and deaths, I marvel at you, Lord. My heart overflows with awe and love . . . I just want to praise and bless you, Lord. Praise you!

Reading: Eccles 8:16-17 & 9:1-7 The business that goes on.

A prayer for myself

Give me, O Lord, a steadfast heart, which no unworthy affection may drag downwards; give me an unconquered heart, which no tribulations can wear out; give me an upright heart, which no unworthy purpose may tempt aside. Bestow upon me also, O Lord my God, understanding to know Thee, diligence to seek Thee, wisdom to find Thee, and a faithfullness that may finally embrace Thee.

St. Thomas Aquinas (1225-1274)

Reading: Wis 7:7-14 & 22-26 In praise of wisdom.

Newman's prayer for unity

O Lord Jesus Christ,
When you were about to suffer,
you prayed for your disciples to the end of time,
that they might all be one,
as you are in the Father,
and the Father in you.
Look down in pity on the manifold divisions
among those who profess your faith,
and heal the many wounds
which the pride of man and the craft of Satan
have inflicted on your people.
Break down the walls of separation
which divide one party and denominations of Christians from another.
Look with compassion
on the souls who have been born in one or another
of these various communions
and bring them all into that one communion
which you set up in the beginning
the one, holy, catholic and apostolic Church.

J. H. Newman (1801-1890)
adapted from his *Meditations and Devotions*

Reading: Jn 17:24-26 That I may be in them.

Learning to pray together

Show me, Lord, what you want me to do to help towards the unity of your body, the Church. I offer myself and my time to you to use as is best.

There is so much talk about how we can grow closer together that I, and many others with me, become confused. Lord, open our hearts, really open them, enlighten our minds so that we may discern your will. Teach us to pray together in a humble, open way so that we grow together at depth and not simply in an intellectual way. We have different mental abilities and can so easily be confused in our minds but we all have hearts; increase our capacity to love you and our fellow Christians; and we have all received your Holy Spirit at baptism, develop in us a greater alertness to his leadings.

Lord help us and guide us in the direction you want us to go.

Amen.

Reading: Phil 2:1-5 Be united in your love.

JANUARY 31

The peace of Christ

The definition of peace is that there should be harmony between two opposed factions. And so, when the civil war in our nature has been brought to an end and we are at peace within ourselves, we may become peace. Then we shall really be true to the name of Christ that we bear.

St. Gregory of Nyssa (*c.* 335-395)
from *On Christian Perfection*

Reading: Lk 1:68-79 The Benedictus.

February

Light struggling with darkness
The beginning of Lent
The experience of the desert

The beginning of February in the season of the Church is the end of the Christmas period. The Presentation of the Lord in the Temple, with the symbolism of light, both scripturally in the words of Simeon and physically in candles, brings us forward in faith to live our lives day by day.

Despite the light, in truthfulness most of us have to accept that we need to live by faith — which is often weak and clouded. We need courage to be, the humility to accept that God loves us even when we fail to love him or each other, the trust to put ourselves unreservedly into his care.

Part of us is likely to know that this has to do with love. With the tip of a finger, as it were, we can sense this love. Then, at another time, it can be deeply overwhelming in its fullness and strength.

The reason is that God is love and it is for him to be present to us as he sees best-suited to the condition of each of us at any given time. Love can be expressed by presence or by apparent absence, by joyous and sweet communication as well as by the giving demand of sheer continuing-to-be-and-to-trust.

However, if we even remotely love, the Church finds a way for us to express this love by giving us the forty days of Lent which most often begins in February. As this commemorates for us the time Jesus spent in prayer and fasting in the desert, we can be led that way also. And the essence of what we are at is a combination of listening to him and making ourselves ready to listen by stripping ourselves of all the encumbrances of living which block out the sound of his voice.

Lent is a time for prayer and penance. The two can be the same for many of us. Let us, then, begin and go forward into Lent with a determination to be open and available for him, through time set aside, through listening to his word in scripture by reading and by sharing in the liturgy. Finally, we can take seriously his advice that some devils can only be thrown out by prayer and fasting.

Whatever else happens towards the end of this month, as we get stuck into Lent let us *really* get stuck in. Each reader is therefore urged to take this admonition seriously, to plan something for the lenten season and to carry it out and through all we say and do and are. Nothing is more public than crucifixion, the witness of Christ to God's love. We, too, are witnessing!

Lighten our darkness

O Lord, thou greatest and most true light, from whence this light of the day and the sun doth spring, O Light, which lightens every man coming into the world; O Light which knowest no night nor evening, but art always a mid-day most clear and fair, without whom all is most dark darkness, by whom things are most splendent; O thou Wisdom of the eternal Father of mercies, lighten our minds that we may only see those things that please thee, and may be blinded to all other things. Grant that we may walk in thy ways this day and that nothing else may be light unto us. Lighten our eyes, O Lord, that we sleep not in death, lest our enemy say 'I have prevailed against him' (Ps 13:3-4); for the sake of thyself, our Lord.

Christian Prayers (1566)

Reading: Ps 36:5-12 In your light do we see light.

The Presentation of the Lord — Candlemas

The most chaste Virgin Mother of God bore in her arms the true light and came to the help of those who were lying in darkness. In the same way we must hurry out to meet him who is truly light, enlightened by the beams of his brightness and bearing in our hands the light which shines for all men.

Indeed this is the mystery which we celebrate, that the light has come into the world and has given it light when it was shrouded in darkness, and that the dayspring has visited us from on high and given light to those who were sitting in darkness. That is why we go in procession with lamps in our hands and hasten bearing lights showing both that the light has shone upon us, and signifying the glory which is to come to us through him. Therefore let us run together to meet God.

That true light which enlightens every man coming into the world has come. Brethren, let us all be enlightened, let us all be filled with light.

St. Sophronius (*c.* 560-638)
from a *Sermon*

Reading: Lk 2:22-28 Story of the Presentation.

A Jewish statement of Faith

Lord help me make my own Jewish statement of faith:
I believe in the sun even when it is not shining.
I believe in love when feeling it not.
I believe in God even when he is silent.

Inscription
on a wall in a cellar in Cologne
where Jews hid from the Nazis

Reading: Ps 55:1-8, 16-18, 22 A prayer in persecution.

FEBRUARY 4

Renew courage in us

Lord Jesus Christ, light shining in our darkness; have mercy on our tired and doubting hearts. Renew in us the courage we need to bring to completion the work your calling has begun in us. Freely you gave your life on the Cross, freely you took it again in your resurrection, you live and reign now, and forever.

Prayer from Taizé

Reading: Ps 27:11-14 I take courage and believe in the goodness of God.

FEBRUARY 5

Let no shadow oppress our spirit

Give unto us, O Lord, the spirit of courage. Let no shadow oppress our spirit, lest our gloom should darken the light by which others have to live. Remove from our inmost souls every root of bitterness, and fill us daily more completely with thy love; through him by whom thou has promised to supply all our need, our Saviour Jesus Christ.

Source unknown

Reading: Ps 27:1-6 The Lord is my light and salvation, whom shall I fear?

FEBRUARY 6

We forget to praise you

Lord, forgive me for not thanking you very often; I seem to forget. You have done so much for us, your creation, yet we forget to praise you. There is the wonder of our own intricate natures and the whole range of the animal kingdom from the flea to the elephant; and there is the amazing way that you have guided mankind to greater knowledge of yourself throughout its long history and the amazing gift of your own Son; and when we are in trouble, you give us love and support. Help me to declare the wonders you do for us, your children, and to thank you for all the blessings which you give to us.

Amen.

Reading: Esther 4:17 & 13:8-17 Mordecai's prayer
or: Dan 2:20-23 Daniel's prayer.

The beams of your brightness

Look upon us, O Lord, and let the darkness of our souls vanish before the beams of thy brightness. Fill us with holy love, and open to us the treasures of thy wisdom. All our desires are known unto thee, therefore perfect what thou hast begun, and what thy spirit has awakened us to ask in prayer. We seek thy face; turn thy face unto us and show us thy glory, then shall our longing be satisfied, and our peace shall be perfect, through Jesus Christ our Lord.

St. Augustine (354-430)

Reading: Ex 34:29-34 The face of Moses shone.

God loves us though unworthy and wandering

O God of love,who hast given us a new commandment through thine only begotten Son that we should love one another, even as thou didst love us the unworthy and the wandering, and gavest thy beloved Son for our life and salvation: we pray thee give us, thy servants, in all the time of our life on earth, a mind forgetful of past ill-will, a pure conscience, sincere thoughts and a heart to love our brethren: for the sake of Jesus Christ, thy Son, our Lord and Saviour.

Coptic Liturgy of St. Cyril.

Reading: Jn 13:34-35 He who loves God should love his brother also.

Fill our hearts with love

O God, the God of all goodness and grace, who art worthy of greater love than we can give or understand: fill our hearts with such love toward thee as may cast out all sloth and fear, that nothing may seem too hard to do or suffer in obedience to thee; and grant that in loving thee we may daily become more like thee and may finally obtain the crown which thou has promised to them that love thee; through Jesus Christ our Lord.

A Pocket Manual of Prayer (1860)

Reading: Mt 11:28-30 By following Christ we learn to love as he loves us.

Help my unbelief

Lord, I believe in thee, help thou mine unbelief. I love thee, yet not with a perfect heart as I would; I long for thee, yet not with my full strength; I trust thee, yet not with my whole mind. Accept my faith, my love, my longing to know and serve thee, my trust in thy power to keep me. What is cold do thou kindle, what is lacking do thou make up. I wait thy blessing, through Jesus Christ our Lord.

Malcolm Spencer

Reading: Mk 9:14-29 I do have faith.

Love took my hand

Love bade me welcome; yet my soul drew back,
    Guilty of dust and sin.
But quick-ey'd Love, observing me grow slack
    From my first entrance in,
Drew nearer to me, sweetly questioning,
    If I lacked anything.
A guest, I answer'd, worthy to be here:
    Love said, You shall be he.
I the unkind, ungrateful? Ah my dear,
    I cannot look on thee.
Love took my hand, and smiling did reply,
    Who made the eyes but I?
Truth Lord, but I have marr'd them: let my shame
    Go where it doth deserve.
And know you not, says Love, who bore the blame?
    My dear, then I will serve.
You must sit down, says Love, and taste my meat:
    So I did sit and eat.

George Herbert (1593-1633)

Reading: Jn 1:29-34 Love, the Lamb of God who takes away
           our sin.

Love is so mysterious

You cannot force love.
Jesus Christ, you did not
Make people love you.
Some were attracted

To you and grew to love you
And followed your way;
Others hated or
despised you.
Love is so mysterious.
The beauty, wisdom or grace
Of a person can awaken something
In another's heart.
I love you; I don't know
How it happened
And I can't explain it;
Somehow I responded to
Your love for me.
How can I inspire others
To glimpse the beauty and wonder
Of you? Show me the way,
I beg you, Lord.

Reading: Mk 10:17-22 Possessions prevent love growing.

When will spring come?

'Those who are sowing in tears will sing when they reap.' A lot of time seems to be spent in digging holes and laying foundations and weeding the garden. I get depressed by this continual putting in and seeming lack of response from the world or you, Lord! How is it possible for me to take a longer look? May it be that what I am doing — what we are doing — will look different later when the spring comes? I hope so, Lord. So often it seems to be winter and mud and toil and no sprouting. But then I think — well, am I not told to live by faith? I trust in the coming of spring, Lord.

Reading: Mt 6:25-34 Do not be anxious.

Lift up your hearts

I consider my own heart and those of all men and reflect on the joy, love and peace of those who consecrate all their faculties to God's service and the contrasting misery, bitterness and unrest with which the world repays her devotee. Then I invite all men living on earth to join me in the zealous service of God, saying: 'O poor, imprisoned human hearts, lift yourself above the walls which enclose you! Wake up, sleeping hearts, throw aside the apathy of your sluggish, careless habits. Take flight heavenward on the

41

wings of a true and complete conversion to the God of all love. Lift up your hearts!'

Henry Suso (c. 1295-1366)
The Exemplar

Reading: Ps 67 Sing for joy.

FEBRUARY 15

Help our weakness

O God, our Father, we are exceedingly frail, and indisposed to every virtuous and gallant undertaking: strengthen our weakness that we may do valiantly in this spiritual warfare; help us against our own negligence and cowardice, and defend us from the treachery of our unfaithful hearts, for the sake of Jesus Christ our Lord. Ancient Prayer

Reading: Jer 17:9-10, 14-18 The heart is deceitful but the Lord can heal it.

FEBRUARY 16

Thine by obedience and love

Thou, O Lord, who commandest me to ask, grant that I may receive; thou hast put me upon seeking, let me be happy in finding; thou hast bidden me knock, I pray thee open unto me. Be graciously pleased to direct and govern all my thoughts and actions, that, for the future, I may serve thee, and entirely devote myself to obeying thee. Accept me and draw me to thyself that I may henceforth be thine by obedience and love, who am already all thine own as thy creature. Even thine who livest and reignest for ever.

St. Augustine (354-430)

Reading: Mt 7:7-14 Ask and it will be given to you.

FEBRUARY 17

Cleanse me from all stains of sin

O that I might praise thee with every faculty of my soul, thou gracious God. That I might thank thee worthily for every manifestation of thy mercy . . . Hallow my soul, and cleanse me from all stains of sin, that the pure sacrifice of my thanksgiving may be pleasing unto thee. Lay hold upon my spirit, and make it a dwelling place for thyself, that I may know thee, and worship thee in spirit and truth. Let thy glory be ever in my mouth, for who is like unto thee, O Lord, thou fountain of all goodness; and who can fully declare thy name? Unto thee belong honour, thanks, and love, who art God from everlasting.

St. Augustine (354-430)

Reading: Ps 51 Praise the Lord, because he forgives our sins, cleanses our hearts.

Reflections on the desert

Lord, we adore your Son as we see him go out into the wilderness alone, away from the bustle of daily life.

He goes to learn your will for him, to discover what kind of Saviour you want him to be.

The desert is empty without tracks and it is easy to get lost; the sky is clear and colours are bright but the very clearness of the air and the light causes mirages, delusions of things not here.

Wild beasts and devils, they say, prowl in the desert ready to catch the unwary; but there are angels too. It is essential to be alert in the desert.

And the desert is a hungry and thirsty place; there is little to eat and it would be more comfortable to go back home where there is food and water.

Being alone in the desert clears the mind, and the heart of man learns to listen and discern what is important in life if the delusions and devils can be overcome.

Your Son went into the desert to discover your will for him, to find how he was to do it, and to count the cost; he was tempted to take easy ways out, sensible ways, worldly ways, but for him the desert was the desert of the love of God, and his only care was to do your will whatever the cost, and the cost, he foresaw, would lead to the death of an outcast on a cross, but he did not shirk it.

Lord, we adore your Son in the wilderness which for him was the wilderness of the love of God.

Reading: Mk 1:9-12 The desert of the love of God.

Forty days and forty nights

Lord, you sent your prophet, Elijah, out into the desert to go to the place of revelation. You made him leave his servant behind; he had to be alone. After one day's journey, he was exhausted and did not want to go on living, so filled was he with his sense of failure. He saw his frailty and sinfulness, but your angel refreshed him and gave him strength to continue. During his long journey, forty days and forty nights, he was tired and hungry, and it was hot by day and cold by night; it was hard to keep going, but you were with him though often he must have doubted this. He learnt to follow your promptings and leadings; he was brave but the cries and howlings of the wild beasts about him and inside him must have been deeply disturbing.

He kept on trusting you and his journey purified his whole being and when he came to your mountain of revelation, he was able to discern your still, small voice.

Lord, we thank you for the lessons the great prophet teaches us.

Amen.

Reading: 1 Kings 19:1-12 Elijah's wilderness experience.

FEBRUARY 20

The need to be alone

Lord, teach us how to recognise our temptations when they come upon us; help us this Lent to find times to be alone with you so that we may learn what you want of us. We are usually so busy doing what we think you want us to do that we rarely take time off to be with you in solitude as Jesus did. The devil so often tempts us to activity and makes us think that this is more important than prayer. Encourage us to try to make time to be alone with you, teach us to pray more deeply, and show us how to give more of ourselves to you to use.

Reading: Mt 6:6 Pray in secret

FEBRUARY 21

Stones into bread

In the wilderness, your Son was tempted to turn stones into bread so as to satisfy the need and hunger of his people in a material way, but he knew that man's deepest hunger is for you. We seem to think that by giving the needy and lonely, food, clothing, better housing, we are doing all we need to serve you in them. But Jesus said 'man does not live by bread alone' — can we satisfy their deepest yearnings when we do not hunger and thirst after you with all our hearts?

Help us to pray more deeply so that we ourselves become more aware of the life of the Spirit, for without this kind of love, we will not be able to teach others about the joy and wonder of living with you.

Reading: Mt 4:1-4 Man does not live on bread alone.

FEBRUARY 22

The temptations by the devil

Lord God, your Son was tempted by the devil to use miraculous gimmicks to convert his people; the Devil suggested if your Son jumped from the pinacle of the Temple your angels would bear him up. But our Lord Jesus knew that to put your power to the test is not faith. Teach us

44

to trust in you and the power of the Holy Spirit and not to resort to gimmicks as a means of converting people to you. Give us the kind of trust your Son had so that we are not always seeking proofs of your power or of your existence. Help us not to fear the consequences of our faith even though we know that your Son's mission led him to the shame and suffering of the cross.

Give us trusting hearts that will not be moved by the changes and upheavals which are rocking the world and the church today.   Amen.

Reading: Mt 4:5-7 We must trust God and not try to test his power.

The temptation of power

Lord God, your Son was tempted in the wilderness to convert the world through the use of political power and through the material display of the kingdoms of this world. We, too, are often tempted to suggest some kind of economic or political revolution as a means of converting others to you. Help us to grow in knowledge of you that we worship you alone and not the ways of the world. Teach us to praise and adore you in a self-forgetting manner so that we learn through coming to know you better the kind of means you want us to use in our mission to the world.

Lord God, you only are holy and we would worship and praise you with our whole being.

Reading: Mt 4:8-11 We must not worship material things.

Generosity in prayer

Almighty God, teach us to pray; teach us to pray in the deep, self-giving way Jesus did in Gethsemane. Like him we acknowledge that all things are possible with you. We know that without you we can do nothing of lasting value. Teach us to begin all our prayer with the acknowledgement of your power and greatness; we so often think that we can do everything on our own and start in prayer with ourselves.

Like Jesus, we put before you what we would like to be done; we would like the world to come to know and love you, and particularly our own small bit of it. Use us for this task; we realize that it will cause us distress and the disturbance of our comfortable lives, and we are afraid. But, Father, if we have to go through with it, your will be done and not ours.

Reading: 2 Thess 1:3-12 That the name of the Lord may be glorified.

FEBRUARY 25

Let only your will be done in me

Father,
I abandon myself into your hands;
do with me what you will.
Whatever you may do, I thank you;
I am ready for all, I accept all.
Let only your will be done in me,
and in all your creatures —
I wish no more than this, O Lord;
Into your hands I commend my soul;
I offer it to you with all the love of my heart,
for I love you Lord, and so need to give myself,
to surrender myself into your hands, without reserve,
with boundless confidence,
for you are my Father.

From *Jesus Caritas*

Reading: Ps 31:1-15 Into your hand I commend my spirit.

FEBRUARY 26

Listening stillness

Teach me how to be quiet,
how to listen to you when you speak
in the silence of the night,
in the silence of my heart.
Teach me how to watch and how to listen
for your still, small voice, in the world,
in others, in myself.   Amen.

Reading: Ps 46 Be still and know that he is God.

FEBRUARY 27

Help me to repent

Isaiah tells us to call on you while you are near. How strange the
Prophet's words are! Surely, Lord, you are always near to us and with us
at all times?

I think I understand; it is we who put ourselves afar off from you
when we sin. We turn away from you and go into a far country. I turn my
back on you when I am angry with others, when I am unforgiving, when I
ride roughshod over the opinions of others, when I hurt people mentally
or physically, when I steal, lie and deceive.

46

Help me to repent and to be sorry when I sin and to realise that I am far away from you. Show me how to return so that I come to live with a sense of your nearness, so that I see you in the wonders of creation, in your loving kindness and goodness to us. Amen.

Reading: Is 55:6-13 Seek the Lord.

FEBRUARY 28

Why do I fear?

The one thing that each person can be completely confident of reaching in life is death, Lord. There is no other complete certainty. Perhaps this is why we so often want to put death out of our minds. For death is too unknown and yet too real a presence — a future state which is dark with anxiety and dread. Yet, you, Lord, are the Lord of life . . . you have promised eternal life. Why then am I restless? Why do I fear? Is it that I do not know you well enough to trust you, well enough to want to give myself into your keeping? Lord teach me today to trust you utterly.

Into your hands, Father, I commend my spirit.

Reading: Rom 7:4-6 We belong to him who was raised from the dead.

FEBRUARY 29

Help me, O God

Help me, O God, to put off all pretence and to find my true self.
Help me, O God, to discard all false pictures of you, whatever cost to my comfort.
Help me, O God, to let go all my problems, and fix my mind on you.
Help me, O God, to see my own sins, never to judge my neighbour and may the glory be all yours.
Into your hands I commend my spirit,
Your will, not mine, be done.

Anthony Bloom
from *Living Prayer*

Reading: Mt 26:36-44 Your will not mine.

March

Making use of Lent
Holy Week and the Passion

In the normal structure of the Church's year, March will always contain a large part of the lenten season. This, then, makes the basis for our way of life during the month.

Lent is a season which has suffered more than most in the recent developments of our world. The easing of penitential exercises and the increase of liberalising provisions has meant that most fasting has disappeared and other types of penitential exercise are little known to the average Christian.

As a way of retaining some of the purpose of the period, the emphasis has been switched in two directions, which are really closely linked. It would be normal today for encouragement to be given for some greater effort to turn our whole selves Godwards by increasing our prayer. We have, therefore, begun the month by thinking a little of what Christ is looking for in us and then we give some days over to various different hints about prayer.

Now, prayer is a vast subject and it is not really entered into by reading or listening to some one talking. Prayer is learnt by practice. More truly, prayer is learnt by living. It would be a wonderful success in our personal lenten development if we consciously gave more time and more of ourselves to God — listening, speaking, thinking, interceding, whether silently in the depths of our hearts or more mentally and vocally.

Regardless of the way we pray, we must not forget that time set aside is important; to be alone with God. This giving of time may indeed be the best penitential exercise or fasting available to us today.

In the variety of our praying, we can ask the Spirit to deepen the knowledge and love of God in our hearts. But we can also spend some time, as Christ did during his life, praying for others. We are always in God's presence. Let us redeem the time this lent.

The other aspect stressed by the Church today is learning more not only from prayer as such, but from study of the Old and New Testaments — with the suggestion that this can be helpfully done in groups which come together to pray and share insights. There can be no better study for us to make towards the end of the month than the unfolding story of the Passion and Death of Jesus Christ. If we learn to share his sufferings then we become more ready to share his glory when we come to the wonder of the Resurrection.

The feast of St. David, Bishop, Patron of Wales

Accept our praise and thanksgiving, O God, for the life and example of Saint David, patron saint of Wales, and grant that following his purity of life and zeal for the gospel of Christ, we may be guided by the Holy Spirit to acknowledge and love you unto our life's end; through the same Jesus Christ our Lord.

Norman Autton

Reading: Is 61:1-4, 10-11 That we may preach the good news.

What true fasting means

Is not this the sort of fast that pleases me —
to break unjust fetters
and undo the thongs of the yoke,
to let the oppressed go free,
and break every yoke,
to share your bread with the hungry,
and shelter the homeless poor,
to clothe the man you see to be naked
and not to turn from your own kin.
Then will your light shine like the dawn
and your wound be quickly healed over.

Isaiah 58:6-8

Reading: Mt 6:16-21 Jesus on fasting.

Christ need not have died

The world has been redeemed by one man's death. Christ need not have died unless he had willed it, yet he did not think a shameful death a thing to be avoided, nor was there any better way to save us than by dying. So his death is every man's life.

St. Ambrose (*c.*340-397)

Reading: Heb 2:10-18 Christ our salvation.

MARCH 4
God in Christ reconciles the world to himself
Being crucified with Christ sound strange; what does it mean Lord? Which part of me must be crucified? Is it the self-centred part which likes to be in control? If this is so, show me how to destroy my self-centredness now. I am discovering how each time I find a way in which I am being self-centred and die to it, I am liberated and have a wonderful sense of freedom. Has this freeing process to be gone through again and again as our ever changing life meets new challenges and as you show us other aspects of our self-centredness? Keep forgiving and liberating me from my self-worship so that I may come to live more fully, freed from the tyranny of self through union with Christ who died that we might live in a new way.

Reading: 2 Cor 5:16-21 In Christ there is a new creation.

MARCH 5
Teach us what to ask for
Lord, we know not what we ought to ask of you; you only know what we need; you love us better than we know how to love ourselves. O Father, give to us, your children, that which we ourselves know not how to ask. We would have no other desire than to accomplish your will. Teach us to pray. Pray yourself in us; for Christ's sake.

François Fénélon (1631-1715)

Reading: Heb 13:20-21 That he may make you ready to do his will.

MARCH 6
Let me be still
Lord, here I am come to pray, but I keep thinking of all the things I have to do today.

Teach me to see that to be before you open and attentive, knowing that you are with me now is the most important thing for me at the moment. The past and future are in your hands, but at this point of time my task is to let the whole of myself be with you, and to accept that this is what you want of me. Let your Holy Spirit make this clearer to me as I offer myself and my time to you, for the sake of your Son Jesus Christ.

Amen.

Reading: Mt 6:31-34 Do not worry.

Our prayer is public

The teacher of peace and unity would not have us pray on our own and in private in such a manner that each prays only for himself. We do not say: 'My Father, who art in heaven', or 'Give me this day me bread'. Each person does not ask for his own sins to be forgiven only, nor does he request for himself alone not to be led into temptation and that he be delivered from evil. Our prayer is public and for all . . . because we are all one.

St. Cyprian (*c*.200-258)
from *On the Lord's Prayer*

Reading: Mt 6:14-15 If you forgive others.

Our Father

What deep mysteries, my dearest brothers, are contained in the Lord's Prayer! How many and great they are! They are expressed in a few words but they are rich in spiritual power so that nothing is left out; every petition and prayer we have to make is included. It is a compendium of heavenly doctrine. 'This is how you must pray', the Lord says.

St. Cyprian (*c*.200-258)
from *On the Lord's Prayer*

Reading: Lk 11:2-5 The Lord's Prayer.

Contemplation

The first step in contemplation is to consider steadily what God wants, what is pleasing to him, what is acceptable in his sight. And since we all make many mistakes and the boldness of our will revolts against the rightness of his, let us humble ourselves under the hand of the most high God: Heal me, O Lord, and I shall be healed; save me and I shall be saved'.

St. Bernard (1090-1153)
from his *Sermons*

Reading: 1 Pet 5:6-7 Be humbled under the mighty hand of God.

Consider how good God is

When we have made some progress in sprirtual exercises, under the guidance of the Holy Spirit, who searches even the depths of God, let us consider how gracious God is, how good in himself. Let us pray with the

prophet that we may see the will of God, and that now we may visit, not
our own heart, but his temple.

St. Bernard (1090-1153)
from his *Sermons*
Reading: Rom 8:5-11 The spiritual are interested in spiritual things.

MARCH 11

Do not be discouraged

The best advice to follow is not to become discouraged and not to stop
praying because you do not get the feeling of devotion you would like...
Our soul is like water that has been agitated. All efforts to quieten it down
will prove of no avail; only time and tranquility will bring back to the
water its original limpidity.

Luis de Granada (1504-1588)
from his *Libro de la Oracion y Meditacion*
Reading: Mk 6:45-52 Jesus walks on the water.

MARCH 12

Do not stand aside, Lord

'My God, my God! Why have you forsaken me?' The psalmist cried out
and was echoed, Lord Jesus, by you as you hung on the cross in agony.
Please teach me when I am in mental, spiritual or physical torment still to
cry out, reaching into blankness in faith. And help me too in listening and
learning from the moments that came after this cry from the cross, when
you said in utter trust: 'Into your hands I commend my spirit, Lord, into
your hands, with trust I do not feel, I commend myself.
Reading: Ps 22 Suffering and Hope.

MARCH 13

To give sight to the blind

I want today to pray for all those who are blind, Lord Jesus. You in your
life were so considerate towards the blind people you met. Give those
who are blind a deepening intelligence so that without eyes they may still
see. Give them sensitivity of ear, a calmness and peace, and above all the
breadth of patience to live fully and without bitterness. I pray too for their
relations and friends that they may always help them. And, for those who
have guide dogs that their dog may be faithful and loving and obedient.
Lord give them sight, if it is your will.
Reading: Mt 20:29-34 Two blind men of Jericho.

For the deaf people in this world

I want today to pray for those who are deaf and hard of hearing. It is easy for me to neglect the deaf person, to get irritated and to find it simpler to avoid contact. I also forget the awful 'cut-offness' of the deaf world from our noisy one. Where would I be without ears to hear speech and music, birdsong and the bark of a dog? Help others to work to help the deaf, Lord. And give deaf people patience, endurance and the strength to learn through signs and lip-reading, that they may become less isolated. Lord cure them if it is your will.

Reading: Mk 7:31-37 Cure of a deaf man.

For the seemingly unbeautiful

We pray to you
for all who have no form or beauty
to look up to,
for those who cannot keep up with others,
for children who have been born unlucky
for all who are disturbed or handicapped,
for those who are incurably ill.
We ask you
that we may discover the meaning
of their presence in this world.

Huub Oosterhuis
from *Your Word is Near*

Reading: Is 49:7-15 I will never forget you.

A prayer of St. Patrick

I will arise today with the power of God to guide me, the might of God to uphold me, the wisdom of God to teach me, the eye of God to watch over me, the ear of God to hear me, the word of God to give me speech, the hand of God to protect me, the way of God to prevent me, the shield of God to shelter me, the host of God to defend me; against the snares of devils, against the temptations of vices, against the lusts of nature, against every man who meditates injury to me, whether far or near, with few or with many.

St. Patrick (c.373-461)

Reading: Is 50:4-9 The Lord comes to my help.

MARCH 17

The feast of St. Patrick, Bishop, Patron of Ireland

Christ with me, Christ before me, Christ behind me, Christ wihin me;
Christ beneath me, Christ above; Christ at my right, Christ at my left;
Christ in my lying down, Christ in my sitting, Christ in my rising up;
Christ in the heart of every man who thinks of me, Christ in the mouth of
every man who speaks to me, Christ in every eye that sees me, Christ in
every ear that hears me. May thy salvation, O Lord, be ever with me.

St. Patrick (*c.*373-461)

Reading: 2 Cor 5:3-10 By the word of truth and by the power of God.

MARCH 18

Go nicely

May God go with you!
Go nicely: may your path be swept of danger.
Let God bear you in peace like a young shoot!
May you meet with the kindly-disposed one!
May God take care of you!
May God walk you well!
May you pass the night with God!
May God be with you who remain behind!
May you stay with God!

John Mbiti
from *Prayers of African Religions*

Reading: Tob 6:2-13 The boy and the angel
or 2 Sam 22:28-34.

MARCH 19

Blaming the system

Today we blame the system; we do not see that people make up and
operate the system. We think if the system were changed there would be
no poverty, injustice, inequality; we do not feel guilty! Lord, we forget
that we are not you! We think that by changing the system all will be well;
we forget that we as individuals are not perfect, and our sins, our failures,
our weaknesses are reflected in the system. Give us each a sense of guilt so
that we may feel the need to change ourselves and to turn from being self-
concerned to being concerned with you and with our fellow creatures.
Lord, change me, and help me to love you more and to care for others as I
do for myself for only through change in us can the system be reformed.

Reading: Rom 6:12-14 Slaves of righteousness.

56

Control of our thought and action

I know that I do, think and say wrong things. It is a daily struggle, Lord, not to do wrong. In this I need your help so much. I understand that you forgive me. I love you for that forgiveness. Thank you. But it would be so nice if I could control my wrongdoing better, rather than always depending on you to forgive. Strengthen me to lead a better life, Lord.

Reading: Rom 12:1-2 Think of God's mercy.

Right and wrong locally and centre

Sin is a word which in former times was used a great deal in the life of the Church. There was much preaching of sin and forgiveness, of the need for repentance. Today, sin is less obvious, morality more blurred and less defined. There is a feeling that it must be right if I want to do it. So, Lord, I am asking you to teach us about good and bad, right and wrong, and help us to live by your truth in your way.

Reading: Rom 7:14-25 Paul on his own difficulties with sin.

Give us an understanding of sin

Thank you for forgiving us our sins. It is difficult for us nowadays to understand what sin is; but sometimes I feel guilty and know that I have failed to respect another person's freedom to choose what they believe to be right. Loving and respecting others is hard; forgive me when I fail and give me greater understanding.   Amen.

Reading: I Jn 4:12-21 Let us love one another.

A prayer to Jesus crucified

Soul of Christ sanctify me,
Body of Christ save me,
Blood of Christ inebriate me,
Water from the side of Christ wash me,
Splendour of the face of Christ illuminate me,
Passion of Christ strengthen me,
Sweat from the face of Christ heal me,
O Good Jesus, hear me,
Within thy wounds hide me,
Suffer me not to be separated from thee,
From the malicious enemy defend me,

In the hour of my death call me,
And bid me to come to thee,
That with thy saints and angels I may praise thee,
For ever and ever. Amen.

Pope John XXII (1249-1334)

Reading: Is 53:1-7 Through his wounds we are healed.

MARCH 24

The cross becomes a cross of glory

The cross has become the common salvation of the whole world.

The cross is called the glory of Christ, and his exaltation: it is the chalice for which he longed, the consumation of his sufferings on our behalf . . . Listen to his words: Now is the Son of man glorified, and God is glorified in him, and God will glorify him at once.

St. Andrew of Crete (*c.* 666-740)

Reading: Jn 13:31-32 Now is the Son of Man glorified.

MARCH 25

Jacob's ladder

When I am overwhelmed by the materialism of today's world, help me, Lord, to remember Jacob's dream of the ladder ascending to heaven with angels coming down and going up from earth to heaven. You made heaven and earth very close, and you have through the life and death and resurrection of your Son made them even closer.

The whole earth provides a taking off place to you if we can but perceive this and let ourselves experience it; even the humblest part of creation is touched by your glory if we keep our eyes open. You are with me now, in this place though I do not understand how; help me to realise that you are with me wherever I go. Amen.

Reading: Gen 28:10-17 You are here.

MARCH 26

Jacob's struggle

Jacob was alone, at night, in the dark valley of the Jabok.

He was afraid of his meeting the next day with his brother Esau,

God told him to go forward into the promised land but Esau barred his way.

He was obedient, and trusted his God — up to a point —

For he took the precaution of sending Esau a handsome present!

Full of uncertainty, he was struggling to understand God's plans,
And then he found himself struggling with the angel of the Lord.
By discovering the angel's name, he hoped to learn more about God and
his ways.
Though Jacob, won, he was wounded and it was God gave him a new
name,
And Jacob learnt more about himself than about his Lord;
Jacob, the coward, was changed and able to face Esau courageously.
Lord, teach me how to face up to my struggles with myself, with others,
with you;
Stop me from evading the difficult, contradictory parts of myself;
Show me how to question you and struggle with you when I find your
ways difficult.
Help me to grow as a person, and to come nearer you through these
conflicts;
Give me courage and strength to do this and do not let me give us!
Reading: Gen 32:22-32 Wrestling with the Lord.

Pilgrims in the wilderness

You called Abraham from his home.
You led the Israelites into the wilderness
where they wandered for many years
before they entered the promised land.
We are in a desert now, not
knowing where you are taking us.
Often we do not know that we are
being led anywhere — we seem to go in circles!
We forget the Spirit who guides us
blows where he wills like the elusive wind
that seems to have no purpose.
We like to see where we are going;
we like security, but you have never
given your people this.
You take everything from us
and we live a hand to mouth existence.
Is this what you want of us?
Will we, like Moses, see your glory
in our wilderness?
Spirit of truth guide us to the Lord
of Glory, to the abiding city.

But as we journey make us aware that you
never leave us comfortless.
Reading: Gen 12:1-8; Ps 107:1-16 & Heb 13:14 Abraham's faith.

MARCH 28

Jeremiah's message

You gave your servant Jeremiah who was a timid man a very difficult message; to announce the destruction of his own country was very bitter to him. He was ill-treated when he preached, but when he tried to keep quiet you were a burning fire in his bones so he could not be silent. You made his life utterly miserable, yet he remained faithful to you.

Give me, O Lord, courage like Jeremiah's so as to live as you would have me do in a world where standards are slipping fast. It is not always easy to be honest in speech or deed for people deride and mock if you are; it is hard to denounce prejudice against race, sex, class. It is easy to shut mind and heart so that we keep your uncomfortable fire out of our bones and being. Show me how I should act and speak, and strengthen me so that I bear the consequences without losing faith in you.   Amen.
Reading: Jer 20 Jeremiah's complaint to God.

MARCH 29

Give us strength

Is it true that if we follow you
we will be hated?
But do we follow you closely enough
to be hated?
Or are we too easy going,
compromising a little here and there
with things that are not really good
but which we cannot believe are really evil?
We do not want to be hated,
and we are surprised when
we meet hatred from others.
Yet you, the Christ, were hated.
Goodness, self-denying goodness,
provokes the hatred of the self-centred,
whether they be in groups or individuals.
Show us how to deny our selfish-selves
and teach us how to love as you love,
even though we may be hated for this.
But give us of your strength

for we do not like being hated and despised.
Reading: Jn 15:18-27 You will be hated as Christians.

Following Christ and taking up the cross

We are reasonable people, Lord, and we know our limitations. You died for us and we feel we need not suffer for you have done all the suffering required; we can carry on living sensibly within our own limitations with no need for heroics or risks of being hurt!

Open our ears so that we hear and understand that you are asking us to take up our cross and to suffer alongside you, with you. Show us that when we refuse injuries, risks, involvement, we are killing you again. Strengthen us so that when the cross for us becomes a serious possibility we do not evade or run away.

When we face up to being involved in your suffering as part of our calling, no doubt we will discover our helplessness — be with us then and support us in our pain, unite our suffering with yours. With your strength help us to bear our sense of inadequacy and failure, and to know that through your cross we will triumph.

Reading: Lk 9:21-25 The cost of discipleship.

The light of the world

O infinite God, the brightness of whose face is often shrouded from my mortal gaze, I thank thee that thou didst send thy Son Jesus Christ to be a light in a dark world. O Christ, thou light of light, I thank thee that in thy most holy life thou didst pierce the eternal mystery as with a great shaft of heavenly light, so that in seeing thee we see him whom no man hath seen at any time.   Amen.

John Baillie
from *A Diary of Private Prayers* (1936)

Reading: Jn 1:1-4 In Christ we see God.

PASSION or PALM SUNDAY

Today, Lord Jesus, you entered Jerusalem in triumph to the 'Hosannas' of the children. As we watch you, we see you reject the kingdom of this world, accepting instead the disgrace of the cross. Help us to understand better the way you look at things, so that your influence on us will influence the world of tomorrow.

Reading: Mat 21:1-17 Entry to Jerusalem.

MONDAY of Holy Week

For some time before your arrest, you were quietly teaching in the temple and living with your friends. As we prepare to commemorate your suffering and death, we ask you for real grasp of your love for individuals both good and bad. Teach us how to love our enemies.   Amen.

Reading: Lk 19:41-48 He taught in the temple every day.

TUESDAY of Holy Week

You came, Jesus Christ, to do the will of your Father and to complete his work. So you taught daily in the temple the good news of repentance forgiveness and love. As we meditate this week on your suffering and death give us the courageous strength to go on preaching and living love when like you we are ignored or rejected.

Reading: Jn 16:25-29 The works of my Father.

WEDNESDAY of Holy Week

Though you must have felt the tension growing, and even noticed the change in Judas, you went calmly about each day, preaching and praying. May your example give us peace and trust in a violent and irreligious world. May your sureness of your Father's love overflow into our hearts.

Reading: Lk 21:37-38 & 22:1-6 Satan entered into Judas.

MAUNDY THURSDAY

Your love is always giving yourself away, Lord God, upon the just and unjust alike. At this last supper of yours, you acted only out of love and later, humbly, sufferingly, you joined your will to your Father's love in the garden. Thank you for the lesson of your love.

Reading: Mk 14:17-42. Last Supper: Gethsemane.

GOOD FRIDAY

In desolation and emptiness, yet still in complete trust you accomplished the will of your Father on the wood of the cross. No one has ever given more of love, more of self. Finally you breathed out the fullness of your gift in love: 'Into your hands I commend my spirit!' Thank you, Jesus.

Reading: Lk 23:33-48 The death of Jesus.

HOLY SATURDAY

Out of darkness — light! For all the centuries of the Old Testament, Lord, your love of Israel remained faithful in their fickleness. Israel forgot you — you loved with an everlasting love. Tonight, rejected yet again, your love triumphs, shining out from the tomb in risen glory. Praise you, Lord. Alleluia.

Reading: Mk 16:1-8 The Resurrection.

EASTER SUNDAY

Believe and rejoice in the Resurrection

The difficulty for our human minds to believe that you rose from the dead tempers our joy. Today we say as deeply faithful as we can be: 'Lord I believe, help my unbelief.' Let our hearts burn within us at the joy of your words.

Reading: Lk 24:13-32 Road to Emmaus.

MONDAY of Easter Week

The feast of the Annunciation

The word of the Lord came to Nathan: Go tell my servant David: Thus says the Lord: You will not build me a house to dwell in . . . but I declare to you that the Lord will build you a house. When your days are fulfilled to go to be with your fathers, I will raise up your offspring after you, one of your own sons, and I will establish his kingdom. He shall build a house for me, and I will establish his throne forever. I will be his father, and he shall be my son: I will not take my steadfast love from him, as I took it from him who was before you, but I will confirm him in my house and in my kingdom for ever and his throne shall be established for ever. In accordance with all these words and in accordance with all this vision, Nathan spoke to David.

1 Chronicles 17:3-15

Reading: Ps 2 You are my son.

TUESDAY of Easter Week

Born in a grave

Your tomb, they say, is empty.

63

Christ is risen, they say.
You are risen indeed, I reply.
Lord, deepen my faith in the new man 'born in a grave'.
Deepen my faith in myself to burst forth from the tomb
    within that is so carefully sealed and guarded.
Deepen my faith, optimism, hope in life.
Deepen our faith in each other, so that we, the church,
so carefully sealed and guarded against the Spirit may
burst open with new life.

Rex Chapman
from A Kind of Praying (1970)

Reading: Lk 24:1-12 The empty tomb.

WEDNESDAY of Easter Week

Where have they put the Lord?

Like Mary Magdalen, I say they have taken away my Lord and I do not know where they have put him. After the joy of Easter I wonder where you are and if your were really raised from the dead. So many people appear to doubt your resurrection that I become bewildered, but, Lord, I have put my trust in you, preserve me and keep me safe. There are so many dangers in my path and so many temptations that I am afraid that I may fall. Hold me up; my life is in your hands.   Amen.

Reading: Jn 20:1-10 Mary Magdalen finds the tomb empty.

THURSDAY of Easter Week

I need your love, Lord

Lord, the story of your meeting with Mary Magdalen in the garden is very wonderful. She needed you and your love so much; I do too. I seem to lose the sense of your presence in my life and I become very sorrowful, and my preoccupation with my loss and its pain blinds me so that I do not see you with me. Then you call me by name and I know that though your appearance has changed, you are close to me. Teach me to realize that after your resurrection you appear to us in many ways and in many places; you are with us in a spring garden, on an ordinary road, at supper or at work. Give me eyes to recognize you and ears to know your voice in every circumstance of life so that I never lose the sense of your presence and your glory.

Reading: Jn 20:11-18 Mary Magdalen meets the risen Christ.

Lord Jesus
    because you rose from the dead,
    a new life is made possible for us.
    You have conquered hatred and jealousy.
    You have conquered sin and death.
    Now you are alive for ever.
    You live to give us your life.
Thank you for the certainty of belief in your resurrection.
Help us to know your transforming power in our daily lives.   Amen.

William N. Richards and James Richardson
from *Prayer for Today*

Reading: Acts 4:5-11 & 33 Faith in the risen Christ heals.

My Lord and My God

Thomas, like us, did not see the empty tomb, and he found it hard to accept the story the other disciples told about your resurrection. You appeared to him and let him see you for himself, and he believed. His cry, 'My Lord and My God!' is so full of worship and adoration that it touches my heart and my soul, and I, too, am driven to my knees in love and worship though I have not seen you with my physical eyes. Help me, Lord, to remember his exclamation when I am bewildered or in doubt.

Amen.

Reading: Jn 20:24-29 Thomas sees the risen Christ.

MOTHER'S DAY

O God of grace and love, in thankfulness for all you have given us through the loving care and hard work of our mothers, we pray for your richest blessing upon all mothers:

For those with difficult homes, whose children are more of a problem than a blessing:

For those with difficult husbands, who find it hard to be constant and loving:

For those with loved ones far away, and those who are lonely:

For those who find it hard to make ends meet, or go short themselves for the sake of their families:

For those mothers who are trying to make Christ real to their families:

For each one according to her need, hear our prayer, and draw all mothers closer to you today, through your son Jesus Christ who greatly loved his own mother.

Christopher Idle (adapted)

Reading: Jn 19:25-27 Behold your mother.

April

The Resurrection
Recognising the risen Lord
'Alleluia'

For any Christian, the central feast of glory and exultation must be Easter, which most often falls in April. At once we celebrate the 'beyond-belief' fact that a man who was put to death appears again. He lives, he moves, he is recognised, he teaches.

So powerful is the force of this new life of Christ that Saint Paul writes to the Corinthians: 'Now if Christ raised from the dead is what has been preached, how can some of you be saying that there is no resurrection of the dead? If there is no resurrection of the dead, Christ himself cannot have been raised, and if Christ has not been raised then our preaching is useless and your believing it is useless.' (1 Cor 15:12-14 [JB]).

In today's debate on Scripture, there are many current ideas and trends which threaten to do what Saint Paul is condemning. But often this is because we human beings, with our fine intellects, feel we should be able to penetrate the veil of mystery which hides God from our sight. This indeed we cannot do, though God himself can lift a corner of the veil for us if he so chooses.

The purpose of our prayer this month centres on the Resurrection, on Easter Day, and all that proceeds from it in revelation: 'But Christ has in fact been raised from the dead, the first fruits of all who have fallen asleep.' (1 Cor 15:20 [JB]).

Because it is so deep a mystery we need to be prepared to sit openly before God, asking him to enlighten us, confident he will, yet clear in our minds and hearts that even the close relations, friends and disciples of Jesus found his appearance after rising from the dead hard to take. He can open our eyes, but we must present ourselves before him in faith, so that he can do so with our free cooperation.

The month then, is filled with rejoicing — rejoicing spiced with wonder, awe, almost incredulity, and intense joy. Our hearts sing 'Alleluia', because there is no way to express the utter glory and praise due to the risen Lord. Doubt lingers, but can be taken up in expressed faith strengthened by the witness of those who were with him after the Resurrection. Their very hesitancy until the inpouring of the Holy Spirit at Pentecost can reassure us that we are not unusual. However, just as they obeyed the command of the risen Lord to wait and pray for the coming of the Spirit, so we can wait, rejoice, share our experience of the wonder and join together in praising, thanking and glorifying God through many an 'Alleluia'.

Philip and the Ethiopian eunuch

Ethiopia was at the end of the world.
Far removed from the thought-patterns of the Jews
He was a modern enough man in his failure to understand the prophet
Yet his sympathies were clear, and he was well on his way to understanding.
The gospel speaks to a man where he is.
There is no need to force the good news down his throat.
Let us be adaptable, Lord.
Let us speak to the point.

Rex Chapman
from *The Cry of the Spirit*

Reading: Acts 8:26-40 Preaching the good news.

Centred on God

If a man is centred upon himself the smallest risk is too great for him, because both success and failure can destroy him. If he is centred upon God, then no risk is too great, because success is already guaranteed — the successful union of Creator and creature, beside which everything else is meaningless.

Morris West
from *The Shoes of the Fisherman*

Reading: Gal 2:20 Christ lives in me.

Make love the motive of my life

Give me thy strength, that thy love may fill my heart, and be the motive of all the use I make of my understanding, my affections, my senses, my health, my time, and whatever other talents I have received from thee. Let this, O God, rule my heart without a rival; let it dispose my thoughts, words, and works; and thus only can I fulfil my duty and thy command, of loving thee 'with all my heart, and mind, and soul, and strength'.

John Wesley (1703-1791)
from *A Collection of Forms of Prayer*

Reading: 1 Jn 3:8-14 The love of God acting in our lives.

Praise for God's goodness and love

Glory be to God in the highest, the Creator, and Lord of heaven and earth, the Preserver of all things, the Father of mercies, who so loved mankind as to send his only begotten Son into the world, to redeem us from sin and misery, and to obtain for us everlasting life. Accept, O gracious God, our praises and thanksgivings for thine infinite mercies towards us. And teach us, O Lord, to love Thee more and serve Thee better; through Jesus Christ our Lord.   Amen.

Gavin Hamilton (1561-1612)

Reading: 1 Jn 4:12-21 The love of God and its demands.

APRIL 5

Seeing the glory of the Son

Teach me to see your glory in your Son as I read the gospels, and to see it as well in your creation as I go about my daily tasks. We do not understand what glory is today but it shines through people and through the beauty of light and sunshine, and in the hills, the sea, the sky. It is there for us to see, open our eyes to it and show your glory too, to others, through us.   Amen.

Reading: Jn 1:14 The glory of the Son.

APRIL 6

Help me always to trust you

My Lord and my Saviour, I love you. You are my preserver and my defence and I know when I am afraid that I can turn to you. I thank you for all your goodness to me; help me to remember to praise you even when things go wrong, and always to trust in your goodness.

Reading: Ps 91 Our hope and strength is in God.

APRIL 7

The light of the Resurrection

Thank you for spring flowers; like your resurrection they bring us hope in a world that seems grim and bleak. There is trouble, sorrow, and violence all around and I come near despair, then I look at the fresh golden yellow of the daffodils and they remind me of Easter. You, who triumphed over all the misery and pain of the crucifixion with its injustice and hate, help us to see in our darkness the golden light of the resurrection with the hope it brings.

Reading: 1 Cor 15:12-20 We hope because Christ was raised from the dead.

Your gift of special peace

Give us that peace which you gave to the disciples after you had been raised from the dead. You gave them a deep peace which sprang from their belief and trust in you and in the power of your Spirit. They were able to go out to tell the world about you and your love for all because they were rooted and grounded in you. Give us that peace which is unshakeable however disturbed the world may be.

Reading: Lk 24:36-49 Christ sends the disciples out into the world to preach the good news.

Burst the bars of fear

As Christians, we have no right to fear and yet we are afraid — of the neighbours, of the people we work with, and even of our own families. Frequently our faith is found behind the locked doors of our hearts. And yet, O Lord, you come to us with peace and the coming is enough to fill our hearts with joy. Burst the bars of fear that keep us silent and send us on your errands, your message not only in our hearts but on our lips. For your name's sake.

Ian D. Bunting
from *Prayers for Today's Church* (1972)

Reading: Jn 20:19 The frightened disciples stay behind locked doors.

Opening our hearts to Christ

I known that you keep knocking at the door of my heart. Sometimes I realise that you are there and let you in for a little time, but then preoccupation with myself and my affairs push you out. Lord, it is spring, the time of rebirth and new beginnings, time for spring cleaning, so come now, today, into my heart, into the centre of my life and remain there. Do not let me drive you out again by my selfishness; take control of my life and stay with me today and every other day.   Amen.

Reading: Rev 3:20 Christ knocks at the door of our hearts.

The joy you promised

Give us the joy which you promised your disciples and which they showed in the world after the death and resurrection of your Son.

Give us the joy, which comes from following him, from knowing that he is the way that leads to you, from knowing that we can trust you completely, from knowing that you love us more deeply than we can love you.

You alone can give us this gift which like your peace passes understanding; realising our unworthiness, but trusting in your generosity, we ask you for this wonderful gift.   Amen.

Reading: Jn 15:9-11 The love and joy God offers.

APRIL 12

Love

Lord Jesus Christ,
You looked down from the cross in love,
  to provide security for your mother,
  companionship for your friend John,
  and forgiveness to those who hated you.
Give us a measure of your perfect love
  and so enable us
to fulfil our obligations to our families,
to show affection and loyalty to our friends,
and to seek reconciliation with those with whom we've quarrelled.

William N. Richards and James Richardson
from *Prayers for Today*

Reading: Jn 15:12-17 Love one another.

APRIL 13

Come alive, Lord

Lord, come alive within my experience,
  within my sorrows and disappointments and doubts,
  within the ordinary movements of my life.
Come alive as the peace and joy and assurance that is
  stronger than the locked doors within with which
  we try to shut out life.
Come alive as the peace and joy and assurance that
  nothing can kill.

Rex Chapman
from *A Kind of Praying* (1970)

Reading: Jn 20:20-23 Jesus appears to the disciples.

APRIL 14

Sing Alleluia!

Here, too, amidst all the dangers and the trials we and others must sing

Alleluia, 'for God is faithful and he will not let you be tempted beyond your strength' as Paul says. So then we must sing here also Alleluia. Man is still a sinner, but God is faithful. Scripture does not say, 'He will not let you be tempted,' but, 'He will not let you be tempted beyond your strength, but with the temptation will also provide the way of escape, that you may be able to endure it'.

St. Augustine (354-430)

Reading: 1 Cor 10:1-13 God is faithful.

APRIL 15

Will you reveal yourself to us?

Lord, we do not always find it easy to recognise you coming to us. Often our spirits are downcast and we, who look for so much in Christ, are frankly disappointed. Will you reveal yourself to us? Open our eyes to undiscovered secrets of your Word. Meet us in the breaking of bread. Set our heavy hearts on fire with love for you and send us on our way rejoicing. For your name's sake.

Ian D. Bunting
from Prayers for Today's Church (1972)

Reading: Lk 24:28-32 The risen Christ eats with the disciples.

APRIL 16

You died in love

O Lord, I see resurrection is bound in with love; you were raised because you died in love; I am raised when, in love, I die to myself. Resurrection gives a new colour to living; the glow of dawn touches my heart and gives me hope and transforms all things and all my relationships with others. It brings hope that I will know you in the sun of paradise. The last dying will bring me to you, the everlasting love and light.

Reading: Song 8:6-7 The quality of love.

APRIL 17

Patience

Few of us, God,
would claim to be very patient.
Patience is a gift of your Holy Spirit,
available to all of us, who ask for it.
Encourage us to seek it,
to find it and to practice it
so that we might work better with other people
and live better with ourselves.

William N. Richards and James Richardson
from Prayers for Today

Reading: Jas 5:7-11 Be patient.

Recognising the risen Lord

I love the picture Saint John paints of you after the resurrection on the shore of the inland sea in the pearly, half-light of dawn when the disciples were out fishing; they saw a figure in the mist but they did not recognise you until you spoke and told them where to cast their net. Then Peter cried out 'It is the Lord' and rushed to you in his usual impetuous way. Open our ears so that we may hear your commands to us and may respond with joy and enthusiasm as Peter did; and forgive us if we do not always recognise you in the early morning fog which so often dims our eyes.

Reading: Jn 21:1-8 Jesus appears to the disciples on the lakeside.

APRIL 19

Recognising the risen Lord

Risen Lord, we thank you for the varied and vivid accounts given to us by those who actually talked with you and ate with you and touched you after your resurrection. We thank you for this visible physical evidence of your power over death. And we thank you, too, for the invisible spiritual evidence which each of us experience in his or her heart, which declares to us that Jesus Christ is still alive. May we, like the first disciples, be brave enough to tell what we have seen and heard so everyone may enjoy the friendship which we have with you and which is our greatest blessing for your name's sake.   Amen.

Patricia Mitchell
from Prayers for Today's Church (1972)

Reading: Acts 2:22-36 Peter preaches the resurrection story.

APRIL 20

You are on the side of mankind

Your reality, your presence is like the pearl of great price Lord. It brings joy, assurance. These urge me to throw everything into a life lived in the knowledge that you are on the side of man, that joy not sorrow is the response to life that you would have a man make.

It urges me to total commitment, even through the lengthy times when you remain as hidden to me as you are to many others.

It is the joy of knowing that life is good at its deepest level, no matter what may befall a man.

Let me communicate this joy to others, Lord.

Let me stake my life on it.

Rex Chapman
from A Kind of Praying (1970)

Reading: Mt 13:44-46 Hidden treasure.

The feast of St. Anselm

Most merciful Lord,
turn my lukewarmness into a fervent love of you.
Most gentle Lord,
my prayer tends towards this —
that by remembering and meditating
on the good things you have done
I may be enkindled with your love.
Your goodness, Lord, created me;
Your mercy cleansed what you had created
from original sin;
Your patience has hitherto borne with me,
fed me, waited for me,
when after I had lost the grace of my baptism
I wallowed in many sordid sins.
You wait, good Lord, for my amendment;
My soul waits for thee in breathing of your grace
in order to be sufficiently penitent
to lead a better life.
My Lord and my Creator,
be my helper.

St. Anselm (1033-1109)

Reading: Ps 30 God our helper and support.

The prayer of St. Richard of Chichester

Thanks be to thee, my Lord Jesus Christ, for all the benefits and blessings which thou has given to me, for all the pains and insults which thou has borne for me. O most merciful Friend, Brother and Redeemer; may I know thee more clearly, love thee more dearly, and follow thee more nearly.

St. Richard of Chichester (+1255)

Reading: 2 Pet 1:2-8 Life in Christ.

The feast of St. George

Lord God, you gave Saint George strength to act bravely and to die an heroic death for the Christian faith many centuries ago; today, in our land, we need the encouragement of his example of fearless witness to the gospel of your Son. Give us courage to fight for what is good and honourable in life, and to put away from us all that is false and mean; make us strong in the power of your Spirit so that in the struggle with evil, we like your great army of heroic saints are more than conquerors through Jesus Christ, our risen Lord.

Reading: Eph 6:10-19 Your strength is in God, put on his armour he gives us.

APRIL 24

God's 'attributes'

You are holy, Lord, the only God,
     and your deeds are wonderful.
You are strong;
You are great.
You are the most High.
You are almighty.
You, holy Father, are
King of Heaven and earth.
You are Three and One,
Lord God, all good
You are Good, all Good, supreme Good,
Lord God, living and true.
You are love,
You are wisdom.
You are humility,
You are endurance.
You are rest,
You are peace,
You are joy and gladness.
You are justice and moderation.
You are all our riches,
And you suffice for us.
You are beauty.
You are gentleness.
You are our protector,
You are our guardian and defender.
You are courage.
You are our haven and our hope.
You are our faith,
Our great consolation.

You are our eternal life,
Great and wonderful Lord
God almighty,
Merciful Saviour.

St. Francis of Assisi (1181-1226)

Reading: Ps 145 Praise of God.

The feast of St. Mark, evangelist

We thank you for your servant John Mark, and the lesson which you teach us through him, namely that you give each of us a unique personal way of witnessing to you. After Mark had failed as a missionary in a wild land, you used him to write of your Son's work of redemption. We thank you for his book that reveals something of the mystery of the son of Man who is also the Son of God if our eyes and ears are open. Help us to search to find the treasure which concealed in this wonderful book and to be alert to the Spirit so that we discover the ways you wish us personally to reveal the good news of your Son.   Amen.

Reading: Mk 8:27-37 Mark's message about the nature of Jesus' Messiahship and the cost of following the Lord.

Lay hold on my spirit

O that I might praise thee with every faculty of my soul, thou gracious God; that I might thank thee worthily for every manifestation of thy mercy ... Hallow my soul, and cleanse me from all stains of sin, that the pure sacrifice of my thanksgiving may be pleasing unto thee. Lay hold on my spirit, and make it a dwelling place for thyself that I may know thee, and worship thee in spirit and truth. Let thy glory be ever in my mouth, for who is like unto thee, O Lord, thou fountain of all goodness, and who can fully declare thy name?

St. Augustine (354-430)

Reading: Ps 147 Give praise and thanks to God.

We must often think of him

We must know before we can love. In order to know God, we must often think of him; and when we come to love him we shall then also think of him often, for our heart will be with our treasure.

Brother Lawrence (Nicholas Herman of Lorraine) (1624-1691)

Reading: Rom 11:33-36 The riches and wisdom and knowledge of God.

Lady Julian's vision

He showed me a little thing, the size of a hazel-nut which seemed to lie in the palm of my hand; and it was round as any ball. I looked upon it with the eye of my understanding and thought, 'What may this be?' I was answered in a general way, thus, 'It is all that is made'. I wondered how long it would last; for it seemed as though it might suddenly fade away to nothing, it was so small. And I was answered in my understanding: 'It lasts, and ever shall last; for God loveth it. And even so hath everything being by the love of God.'

Lady Julian of Norwich (1342-*c*.1412)

Reading: Is 41:8-10 The Lord holds us in his hand.

The feast of St. Catherine of Siena

Christ is the bridge from Time to Eternity. The road to heaven was broken down by the Fall; 'Wherefore', said the Divine Voice, 'I have made a Bridge of my only begotten Son . . . But it is not enough that My Son should have made you this bridge unless you walk thereon.'

The soul must make some effort itself; it must mount the three steps which lead to the crown of the Bridge; and it mounts through Love, 'for Love carries the soul as the feet carry the body'.

St. Catherine of Siena (*c*.1347-1386)
from *Divine Dialogue*

Reading: 1 Thes 3:11-13 May Christ make it easy.

The risen Christ is object of our joy

This lasting joy which no power on earth can take from the disciples is not confined to the passing appearances. The risen Christ is the object of the joy, the appearances mark the beginning of it. What guarantees its perpetual continuance is the actual possession of the glorified Christ through the agency of the Holy Spirit, to which will be added the direct vision in the eternal kingdom.

Alfred Loisy (1859-1940)

Reading: Jn 16:20-22 No man can take your joy from you.

May

Service
The difficulties of parting
The Holy Spirit and the Holy Trinity

Because of Easter falling in late March or April the month of May can be a very rich one with the climax of the Paschal season leading on to Pentecost and Trinity. Accepting that most often Easter falls in April, this means that May usually includes all this richness for us, though it is possible in some years for there to be an overlap into June.

But it is not only that main richness. Traditionally the first day of May has always been some kind of a celebration until it has turned in more recent times to a kind of Labour Day. And in addition, some parts of the Church have given a special place to devotion to the Virgin Mary during the whole month.

While taking note of these more devotional aspects which can be said to draw attention to the service of mankind for the Gospel and the world, the main emphasis should be on the intensely spiritual message of the sending of the Holy Spirit.

This begins with the sad-gladness of Jesus going back to his Father in Heaven at the Ascension. The pain of parting cuts deeply, even when we know in our hearts that the one we love is going to peace and joy. A sense of loneliness as well as joy perhaps held the apostles as they waited in prayer with the Virgin Mary as Jesus had told them to do.

So we have a good opportunity for opening ourselves before and during the Pentecostal period to the inpouring of the Holy Spirit. The Lord wants us to be full of faith and hope in the Spirit's presence and power. Those who have already been awakened by the reality of the Spirit and felt his gift will be full of praise and thanksgiving and renewed expectation. For others who are still less touched by the Spirit of Jesus this period can be one of calm, open and deeply hopeful waiting to be taken by the power of God into a new richness of spiritual expectation. Here it is important that we should all realise the work of the Spirit as being by far the larger part. Our part is to come, to be ready, to expect his presence, and to praise and glorify God. The actual inpouring is God's work on the receptive heart.

With the coming of the Spirit, the disciples knew Jesus in a different way, and were given strengh, power and courage to go out and preach the Gospel. This they were able to do with wonderful results. If we are generous in the gift of ourselves in prayer and living, we too are promised power beyond anything we can imagine or personally achieve. The source of this power is the Holy Trinity — God revealed and yet still too vast and deep a simplicity for us to grasp with the mind. This great season should take us tranquilly and contemplatively into prayer of the heart, from which will emerge in our lives the Word our lives should speak.

May Day: the feast of St. Joseph the worker

There is a long history, both pagan and Christian, Lord, of using the first day of May as a time for festivity. More recently it has been a rallying point for workers of the world and so part of the Christian Church now thinks in a special way of Saint Joseph. While we admire the humility of Joseph and the traditional sense of his working to support his family of Mary and Jesus and himself, we ask you that his example may go deep into the minds and hearts of all of us who are living in this world. May we learn the responsibility of work, the right relationship of employer and employee, the essential justice of wages, conditions, hours of work; the imperative need to fight unemployment; the good use both of money we earn and the hours of leisure that we have. Keep us centred on the love and unity which builds family and neighbourhood, so that there is peace in our hearts, peace in our homes and peace on the streets. Let us appreciate and not despise each other.

Reading: Lk 4:23-30 The son of Joseph.

The authority of God

By thy leave, O Lord, from ore and mine, in furnace and foundry, with lathe and bore, we shape our tools and take our powers. Civilization through metallurgy, culture by electronics, iron and the soul. Grant us, we pray thee, so to wield power as to learn reverence, so to take the force that we may bow to the mystery of nature, so to yield to thy authority that we rightly know our own.

Kenneth Cragg
from *Alive to God* (1970)

Reading: Job 38:1-38 God alone created and controls nature.

The feast of St. Philip and St. James, apostles and martyrs

Lord Jesus Christ, Philip knew that you were someone special and he brought Nathaniel to you, and the Greeks who wanted to see you came to him for an introduction; yet Philip did not understand until the Last Supper that you are the way to God the Father, and that he who has seen you has seen the Father. Philip and James preached this, your gospel, and were put to death for it. Help me to understand more clearly the revelation you made to Philip. Reveal yourself to me more plainly so that understanding you a little better I may see something of the glory of God, your Father. Amen.

Reading: Jn 14:6-14 is the way to God the Father whom he reveals to us.

MAY 4

Communicating the Good News of the risen Christ

When people are all around us, Lord,
And we see their unseeing eyes and know them to be lost in their private
    world.
Unable to see a sparrow die:
Lord, help us to communicate.
Break through the barriers of men's minds:
Help us, Lord, to help each other with the gospel
of the risen Lord, that every race be friends for his name's sake.

Susan Heywood
from *Prayers for Today's Church* (1972)

Reading: Acts 2:4-6 The Holy Spirit makes understanding possible.

MAY 5

Faithful stewards

O God, whose dear Son Jesus Christ, earned his bread at Nazareth by the labours of his hands, and taught us that our possessions are a trust from you; help us to be faithful stewards of what you give us; that in earning we may be just and honest, and in spending we may not look for our own glory but yours and for the good of others; through the same our Lord Jesus Christ.

A New Prayer Book (1923)

Reading: 1 Pet 4:7-11 Be faithful stewards.

MAY 6

Parting

Life is full of partings, a daughter or a son leaves home to work or get married, friends and lovers often have to separate for long times, and

82

death would seem to be the last parting. Help us to see that because we have your Spirit in us, we are linked one with another through you, and that we can never be separated from you or them. But we are human, and partings are always sad and painful; the disciples did not want you to leave them and go to your Father, yet after you had gone you did not leave them comfortless; you gave them fullness of life through the Holy Spirit. Give us a deeper sense of the presence of your Spirit and a fuller experience of the communion of saints.

Reading: Acts 1:4-11 Jesus leaves his disciples.

Strengthen us against the pain of parting

Lord, in your life on earth, you knew all about parting; you had to leave your home and your family and its stability to go into a wider world to preach your good news; you had to part company with the establishment of your time; your closest friends left you when death threatened; and Judas, one of them, betrayed you to your enemies. You certainly knew about partings but you were not overwhelmed by them; in love you went through them though they must have been painful. Strengthen us so that when painful partings occur in our lives, we will know you are supporting us and that if we trust, our prayer will be deepened through our pain. And through our experience of your closeness and love, help us to assist others when they are experiencing the grief of parting.   Amen.

Reading: Jn 19:25-28 Jesus parting with his mother and Saint John.

The silence of God

Lord, I am sinful and I need your help, but you seem to be leaving me alone. There is just silence, a kind of emptiness in my heart; I know spiritual writers say we are nearest you in silence, and in stillness; 'nothing in all creation is so like God as stillness!' In stillness and aloneness, I become so aware of my littleness and helplessness; I realize that we need love and trust to find you in stillness. O Jesus Christ, who are the way to God, the Creator, the Lord of stillness, guide me, take me to your Father and peace and forgiveness.   Amen.

Reading: Jer 32:37-44 I mean to gather them.

Christ the mediator

First of all, we should note that to conclude our prayer we say 'through

Jesus Christ your Son our Lord', but never 'through the Holy Spirit'. It is not for nothing that the Catholic Church is united in this practice which is founded on the mystery that the man Jesus Christ was made mediator between God and men, priest for ever after the order of Melchizedek, who, taking his own blood, entered once for all into the Holy Place not made with hands, a copy of the true one, but into heaven itself where, at the right hand of God he intercedes for us.

St. Fulgentius of Ruspe (486-533)
from his *Letters*

Reading: Heb 4:14-16 & 5:1-3 The supreme high priest.

MAY 10

Hidden God

God, hidden from our eyes,
Man have always been searching for you.
We probe the distance of space;
We plumb the depths of our own minds.
We find you, but never completely.
Left to ourselves we should go on searching for ever.
Only you can bring our search to its goal.
But you have done that:
You have revealed yourself to us in Jesus Christ.
As a baby he was born in a stable in Bethlehem;
As a man he died on a cross at Calvary.
In him our search has reached its goal.
God, hidden from our eyes.
God, hidden from our eyes,
Yet revealed in Jesus Christ,
We worship and adore you.

Caryl Micklem
from *More Contemporary Prayers*

Reading: Acts 17:22-32 Paul reveals the unknown God.

MAY 11

You are Lord

You are not only risen and alive, you are Lord.
This is your ascension, your ascendancy over the whole universe.
You stand over and above all that is best in life as its source.
You stand above all that is worst as ultimate victor.
You stand above all powers and authorities as judge.

You stand above all failure and weakness and sin as forgiveness and
   love.
You alone are worthy of total allegiance, total commitment.
You are Lord,
My Lord and my God.

Rex Chapman
from *A Kind of Praying (1970)*

Reading: Acts 1:1-11 Jesus' Ascension.

We can ascend to God

Almighty and merciful God, into whose gracious presence we ascend, not
by the frailty of the flesh, but by the activities of the soul: make us ever by
thine inspiration, to seek thy courts of the heavenly city, whither our
saviour Christ hath ascended, that by thy mercy we may confidently enter
them both now and hereafter; through the same Jesus Christ our Lord.

Leonine Sacramentary (early 7th century)

Reading: Ezek 1:4-5 & 26-28 The glory of God.

Learning to be redundant

Jesus, our teacher and example, in three years you trained the disciples
for their work and then left them with the uncomfortable power of the
Holy Spirit. Help missionaries and others to learn to be redundant, to
know how to train and teach others, to know when to hand over and
move on. Help them to get out gracefully when their work is done, for
you yourself became redundant for the good of the Church.

J. Wheatly Price
from *Prayers for Today's Church* (1972)

Reading: 1 Cor 3 We may plant but, only God gives the growth.

Being open to the demands of the Spirit

Holy Spirit, Lord God, giver of life, come to us as a refreshing and
   strengthening power.
Purge out of our lives all that denies your inspiration.
Keep us alert to your challenges.
Let us be open to your new demands in the world and in the church.
Give us humility that we may see the vision, and trusting in your power
   may commit ourselves to it, in the name of Christ our Lord.

Brother John Charles, SSF
from *Contemporary Parish Prayers*

Reading: 1 Cor 12:4-11 The Spirit works in different ways.

Waiting for the Spirit

Trusting in thy word, O Lord, we wait for thy Spirit. Send him forth from thy holy heaven, to sanctify our hearts, our deeps, which without him are empty and without form. Give us grace to remain humble and still under his action. Quicken us, O Lord, according to thy loving kindness.

Evelyn Underhill (1875-1941)
from *Prayers and Meditations*

Reading: Eccles 2:1-23 Cling to him and do not leave him.

MAY 16

Come, Holy Spirit

O God, the Holy Spirit,
Come to us, and among us:
Come as the wind, and cleanse us;
Come as the fire, and burn;
Come as the dew, and refresh:
Convict, convert, and consecrate
many hearts and lives to our great good
and thy greater glory, and this we ask
for Jesus Christ's sake.

Eric Milner-White (1884-1963)

Reading: Joel 2:28-29 I will pour out my Spirit on all mankind.

MAY 17

The Spirit and prayer

Most Holy Spirit, Comforter,
the ever present guest within the soul
the voice of conscience
the call to holiness
the strength that holds the will
if it convert
and turn from self to godliness:
thou art most close, most intimate,
bring me to quietude
that I may hear within my soul
what thou dost say.
It is my restless self-absorption,
my undisciplined approach to outward things,

my fears, my hopes,
that dull the hearing of my soul
that make me dread the silence
  wherein thy voice is heard.

Gilbert Shaw
from *A Pilgrim's Book, Six Prayers* (1945)

Reading: Rom 8:22-27 The Spirit helps us pray.

Waiting with love in our hearts

Father in heaven, thou hast loved us first, help us never to forget that thou art love so that this sure conviction might triumph in our hearts over the seduction of the world, over the inquietude of the soul, over the anxiety for the future, over the fright of the past, over the distress of the moment. But grant also that this conviction might discipline our soul so that our heart might remain faithful and sincere in the love which we bear to all those whom thou has commanded us to love as we love ourselves.

Søren Kierkegaard (1813-1855)
from *The Prayers of Kierkegaard*

Reading: Jn 3:16-21 God loves us.

Waiting in silence

Teach us, O Spirit of God, that silent language which says all things. Teach our souls to remain silent in thy presence: that we may adore thee in the depths of our being and await all things from thee, whilst asking of thee nothing but the accomplishment of thy will. Teach us to remain quiet under thy action and produce in our soul that deep and simple prayer which says nothing and expresses everything, which specifies nothing and expresses everything.

J. N. Grou (1731-1803)
from *How to Pray*

Reading: Ps 62:1-7 For God my soul waits in silence.

Not worthy

Lord, I am not worthy
that thou shouldst come under my roof,
yet I know that I cannot live without thee;
Lord, I am sinful;
without thee I cannot become holy.

Lord, I am unloving;
come to my heart and waken it to love.
Lord, my heart is so small;
enlarge it and throw it open,
that I may welcome thee and make room
for all who come looking for love.

George Appleton
from One Man's Prayers

Reading: Lk 7:1-10 Cure of the centurion's servant.

MAY 21

The footfall of an ant

Pray unto him in any way you like. He is sure to hear you, for he can hear even the footfall of an ant.

Ramakrishna (1836-1886)

Reading: Wis 7:15-21 He gave me knowledge of all that is.

MAY 22

Redeemed by the death of Christ

God Almighty, you sent Jesus Christ into the world of men and women and children so that he might teach us that love covers a multitude of sins. He called and still calls each one of us to repentance, though we do not always even recognise our sins. Teach each of us today as we stand before you as sinners who are redeemed by the death and resurrection of Jesus. Teach us to be grateful for this generous love of his and to learn to respond in obedience to that love, as each of us still later stand before your judgment seat, O God, and be judged by love.

Reading: Rom 5:17-21 By one man's obedience.

MAY 23

I know my redeemer lives

In the middle of the turmoil of this life, it is easy for me to lose hope in you, Lord. I look at myself and see my repeated failures. I look at others and so often recognise greed and envy, violence, selfishness and pride. I know then deep down how badly I need redemption. I know too that 'my redeemer lives'. But in stress and seeming hopelessness the whole thing gets out of focus. I lose you Lord. I lose the sense of Christ's saving power. All around I see only evil conquering, violence growing, greed advertised as necessary for everyone. Give me a right vision, Lord; give me hope that I may say and mean and live with deep conviction the certainty that my redeemer lives.

Reading: Rom 5:5-11 Hope is not deceptive.

My soul is shut out from peace

It is easy to despair when I find that 'my soul is shut out from peace'. The daily news appals me. Whenever I switch on the television I see hijacking, murder, war, robbery and a hundred other things. Is there never any cheerful news in your world, Lord? Are we really living on the edge of hell, where greedy selfishness becomes our god. Jesus Christ promised peace . . . but where is it? It is neither in the world nor in my heart. Give me new hope and trust in you. You alone can save me from myself and give me hope.

Reading: Lam 3:17-26 Wait in silence for the Lord to save.

How we should pray

What then is devotion? One must free his heart from all other thoughts and regard himself as standing in the presence of God. Therefore, before engaging in prayer, a man ought to go aside for a little in order to bring himself into a devotional attitude, and then he should pray quietly and with feeling, not like one who carries a weight and goes away. Then after prayer the worshipper ought to sit quiet for a little and then depart.

Moses Maimonides (1135-1204)

Reading: Phil 3:20-21 Our homeland is in heaven.

Make me free

I am not free, Lord.
You gave me freedom,
creating me to your image and likeness.
But I have lost your likeness and my freedom
day after day, little by little.
I have lost my freedom by removing myself from you,
separating myself from my brothers and sisters
and entrenching myself in pride and selfishness.
I have given myself to sin
and become the servant of evil.
Deliver me, Lord.
Deliver me, Lord,
and draw me close to you
and my brothers and sisters,
so there I shall be more free.
Lord, make me free.

Anonymous

Reading: Gal 5:13-15 We are called to freedom.

God is beyond any description of ours

O God above all things
(what other name describes you?)
What words can sing your praises?
No word at all denotes you.
What mind can probe your secret?
alone beyond the power of speech
all men can speak of springs from you;
alone beyond the power of thought
all men can think of stems from you.
All things proclaim you —
things that can speak, things that cannot.
All things revere you —
things that have reason, things that have not.
The whole world's longing
and pain mingle about you.
All things breathe you a prayer,
a silent hymn of your own composing.

St. Gregory Nazianzen (329-395)

Reading: Rom 11:33-36 The unsearchableness of God.

MAY 28

Have mercy upon us

Have mercy upon us.
Have mercy upon our efforts, that we
Before thee, in love and in faith,
Righteousness and humility,
May follow thee, with self-denial,
Steadfastness and courage,
And meet thee in the silence.
Give us a pure heart that we may see thee,
A humble heart that we may hear thee,
A heart of love that we may serve thee,
A heart of faith that we may live thee.

Dag Hammarskjöld (1905-1961)
from Markings

Reading: Ps 85 Show us your steadfast love.

MAY 29

Adoration

God the Father, God beyond us, we adore you.

You are the depth of all that is.
You are the ground of our being.
We can never grasp you, yet you grasp us;
the universe speaks of you to us, and your love comes to us
through Jesus.

God the Son, God beside us, we adore you.
You are the perfection of humanity.
You have shown us what human life should be like.
In you we see divine and human greatness combined.

God the Spirit, God around us, we adore you.
You draw us to Jesus and the Father.
You are the power within us.
You give us abundant life and can make us the men and women we
are meant to be.

Father, Son and Spirit;
God, beyond, beside and around us;
We adore you.

From *Contemporary Prayers for Public Worship*

Reading: 1 Jn 5:6-12 Divine witness.

Glory and worship

Mole felt a great Awe fall upon him, an awe that turned his muscles to
water, bowed his head, and rooted his feet to the ground. It was no panic
terror — indeed he flet wonderfully at peace and happy — but it was an
awe that smote and held him and, without seeing, he knew it could only
mean that some august Presence was very, very near . . . he raised his
humble head; and then, in that utter clearness of the imminent dawn,
while Nature, flushed with fullness of incredible colour, seemed to held
her breath for the event, he looked in the very eyes of the Friend and
Helper . . . 'Rat!' he found breath to whisper, shaking, 'Are you afraid?' . . .
'Afraid! Of *Him*. O, never, never! And yet — and yet — O, Mole, I am
afraid!' Then the two animals, crouching to the earth, bowed their heads
and did worship.

Kenneth Grahame (1859-1932)
from *Wind in the Willows*

Reading: Is 6:1-5 The holiness of God and unworthiness of man.

In praise of God

Holy, Holy, Holy, Lord God Almighty!
Early in the morning our song shall rise to Thee;
Holy, Holy, Holy! Merciful and mighty!
God in Three Persons, Blessed Trinity!

Holy, Holy, Holy! though the darkness hide Thee,
Though the eye of sinful man Thy glory may not see,
Only Thou art Holy, there is none beside Thee
Perfect in power, in love and purity.

Holy, Holy, Holy! Lord God Almighty!
All Thy works shall praise Thy name, in earth, and sky and sea.
Holy, Holy, Holy! Merciful and Mighty!
God in Three Persons, Blessed Trinity!

Bishop Reginal Heber (1783-1826)

Reading: Is 40:29-31 He is the everlasting God.

The Ascension

O Risen Saviour, bid me rise with thee
and seek those things which are above;
not only seek, but set my whole heart upon them.

Thou art in heaven, ever raising lives to thyself;
O, by thy grace, may mine be making that ascent
not in dreams, but in truth,
now, tomorrow, always.

Daily in spirit, in thy Holy Spirit,
Let me behold thee on the throne of God,
Thou king reigning in holiness,
Thou conqueror of all evil,
Thou majesty of love,
very God and very Man,
of glory unimaginable and eternal
in whom all hope is sure.

Eric Milner-White (1884-1963)
from *My God, My Glory* (1954)

Reading: Lk 24:50-53 Jesus ascends.

Spirit of joy

Holy Spirit, giver of joy, touch our hearts with your joy. It is so easy for us to get depressed, dulled and dreary. Then we can give Jesus and his followers a bad name, because we appear to gain nothing from what you pour out upon us. Make our faces shine with joy so that others may take heart through us and grow in your love.

Reading: Phil 4:4-9 Always happy in the Lord.

TUESDAY before Pentecost

Spirit of love

Spirit of love, flow into our minds and hearts. May our whole being drink you in. From your love may our love grow, until each of us can overflow with that love as a free gift to others. Generous Spirit enrich the world with the warmth we so sorely need, that our hardness and lack of response is melted into a union of affection and care for each other, and especially those who seem to be unloved.

Reading: 1 Cor 13:4-8 Love.

WEDNESDAY before Pentecost

Spirit of peace

Jesus promised the peace the world cannot give — your gift of peace to me. Holy Spirit, give me peace in my heart that I may be truly open in my trust of you. Give me tranquility of bearing, so that I may spread your peace among those I meet. And, Holy Spirit, give peace to this warring world of men, women and children over whom you brood with love.

Reading: Jn 14:16-21 A peace the world cannot give.

THURSDAY before Pentecost

Spirit of truth

Spirit of truth, lead us into all truth. This was the promise Jesus made, please now fulfil that promise by helping us to know the truth of the Good News of Jesus so deeply and so movingly that it may radiate around us to touch the minds and hearts of men. Tell us of the first priority of love. Tell us how to see the different shades of right and wrong, and how to have the strength to follow the true way. Holy Spirit teach us Jesus who is the truth and the life.

Reading: Jn 14:16-21 The spirit of truth.

Spirit of patience

You love with an everlasting love because you are love. And so you are patiently effective always and everywhere, even when we cannot feel your presence. Teach us to love without wanting to control; to love without limit; to love you, our friends and also our enemies. Teach us to be patient in love when love is not returned; teach us to be patient when even you are apparently far away. Teach us loving, waiting patience when there is no answer to my questioning and my doubt.

Reading: Jn 14:8-11 You still do not know me?

Benign Spirit

Benign Spirit, warm and smile upon my heart. My whole being cries out for love and comfort, while at the same time I know that I serve Jesus and him crucified. It is for you to reconcile these opposite poles of my senses . . . comfort and love against persecution and the way of the cross. Bring them into harmony in me so that I may myself be warm and compassionate to those who come close to me today, to those who cross my path and with whom I might naturally quarrel and be at odds. O benign Spirit, make me a kindly and comforting person.

Reading: Lk 15:11-32 The Prodigal son.

Pentecost — The coming of the spirit

Holy Spirit of God, you came upon Mary at Nazareth and so filled her that she gave birth to the Son of God and called him Jesus. We ask you at this time to fill our minds and hearts, the whole of our being, that we in our turn may bring forth your Word to the waiting world.

Reading: Lk 1:31-36 You shall conceive a son.

Father most holy, merciful and tender;
Jesus our Saviour, with the Father reigning;
Spirit of mercy, Advocate, Defender,
Light never waning.

Trinity sacred, Unity unshaken;
Deity perfect, giving and forgiving,
Light of the angels, life of the forsaken,
Hope of all living.

Maker of all things, all thy creatures praise thee;
Lo, all things serve thee through thy whole creation
Hear us, Almighty, hear us as we raise thee
Hearts adoration.

To the almighty triune God be glory:
Highest and greatest, help thou our endeavour;
We too would praise thee, giving honour worthy,
Now and for ever.

Anonymous prayer (10th century)
translated by Percy Dearmer

Reading: Is 43:1-7 Do not be afraid.

The feast of Corpus Christi — the body of the Lord

Lord Jesus, on the night before you suffered, you asked your friends to a meal. At this you offered prayers, you gave a wonderful sermon on unity and love, you showed your humility and your care by washing your disciples'feet. Was this not enough to convince us of your love? Well, you are *Lord,* and evidently you thought it was not enough, because the next thing you did was to say those mysterious words: 'Take, eat, this is my body' — 'Take, drink, this is the cup of my blood'.

And now for a very long time, Lord Jesus, there has been dispute about this wonderful thing you did. Your Last Supper and your dying on the Cross have become the centre of Christian worship. But since the fragmenting of Christendom, there have been different understandings of what you meant by your words.

Please, Lord Jesus, help all Christians to come somehow to an acceptance which takes all varieties of understanding into account and yet enables us all to take and eat as you have commanded.

Further, Jesus, open the minds and hearts of those who do not even accept you as God and Man, to grasp the power of what you have given and to respond by acceptance which is at once vibrant and tranquil. In this way, may all mankind come to your love.

Reading: 1 Cor 11:23-27 What I received from the Lord.

June

The life of the Church in Eucharist
Martyrdom
The cheerful loving service of the saints

After Pentecost and Trinity, the liturgical life of the Church settles down (if that is the right word) to the ordinary humdrum of the weekly round. Apart from individual highlights of feast days, there is no new Church season until once more we come round to Advent.

June, then, we can allow to emerge for us as the day to day pattern of living with the Lord, who is always with us, and yet can so easily be forgotten in the hundred and one cares of the world.

Most often it is during this month that we celebrate the feast of Corpus Christi. This may immediately take some of us into the difficulty of Church membership, because it brings to the fore the whole long theological and historical debate about the presence of Christ in the Eucharist. Without trying to clarify the issue here, we can face it. Facing it, we can pray that the Eucharist which *should be* the central unifying act of worship for all Christians may soon in God's providence *become so* once again, rather than being a point of acute pain and division, as it has been now for many centuries. Unless we are all prepared to face the pain and to work and pray for growing-together of the differing traditions, our prayer for unity according to Christ's will, which we stress in January, can easily become a mouthing of empty words.

We speak of the day by day pattern of living in the Church, and the Eucharistic crisis of conscience has in the past led to martyrdom for some. And so it is not surprising that the scattering of saints' days during the month of June gives us a colourful backcloth. Whether we start at the end of the month with those two great pillars of the Church, Peter and Paul, or go even further back to John the Baptist, or come forward in

99

time to the great Englishman, Thomas More — we find the same thread of utter giving-of-self-to-God which characterises martyrdom as a definite and continuous pattern of life in the Church. More recently, Ugandans of differing Christian allegiances bore the same witness, and we are by this commemoration brought strongly into the present day. We should all be aware that men, women and children are dying in our own age for the beliefs for which they stand. Martyrdom has not come to an end but is horrifyingly real today.

However, not everyone who is recognised, whether officially or popularly, as a holy or saintly person is necessarily proved by martyrdom. For many, working out life is in taking up the cross daily and following Jesus, without anything very dramatic happening, except that they manage in a quiet way to radiate the cheerfulness, tranquility, hope, love and service which are redolent of true Christianity.

Take me over

My Lord and my God,
  take me from all that keeps me from you.
My Lord and my God,
  grant me all that leads me to you.
My Lord and my God,
  take me from myself and give me completely to you.

Nicholas of Flue (1417-1487)

Reading: Phil 3:7-11 Paul suffered the loss of all things for Christ.

Prayer across the world

Show me, Lord, how I ought to be praying for my fellow Christians on other continents. They, like me, are part of the Body of Christ, and I am ashamed that I am learning so little about how to rejoice with them, how to weep with them.

A missionary in Africa a long time ago wrote home: 'It is so difficult here in these dark forests to touch the hem of his garment.' Today, only you, know the identity of the thousands of African Christians, who are trying desparately to hold on to you or even to touch the fringe of your love.

Lord, encourage them all with a reminder of what you have done for their peoples. Help Ugandans who must ask, 'Why? Why?' when they think of the recent centenary year of their country's first Christian martyrs — and the new martyrdoms today. Help to drive away bitterness about the past and give them trust, and hope, for the future.

Open my ears, Lord, to listen with understanding to this call from overseas, 'Brethren, pray for us!'

Joyce Chaplin

Reading: Ps 94 The Lord will not abandon his people.

The feast of the Uganda Martyrs

In Uganda about a hundred years ago Catholic and Protestant Christians shared in their witness to you, Lord, and died bravely for your gospel; and today Uganda still provides her martyrs, yet her church is praising you at present with a deeper joy than probably we shall ever know. Give us, divided Christians, who share the same Spirit the desire and courage to witness to our common love for you in an increasingly pagan world, and give us the joy of heart which will lead us to praise you whatever happens; and above all keep us praying for our persecuted fellow Christians, particularly at this time, for those in Africa.   Amen.

Joyce Chaplin (adapted)

Reading: Mk 13:5-13 You will be beaten in synagogues.

JUNE 4

Make us holy saints

O God, our Father, we are helpless without your help.
> Unless you help us,
> We can see the ideal,
> but we cannot reach it.
> We can know the right,
> but we cannot do it.
> We can recognise our duty,
> but we cannot perform it.
> We can seek the truth,
> but we can never wholly find it.

All our lives we are haunted by the difference between what we ought to do and what in fact we can do.
> By your Holy Spirit,
> Enlighten our minds,
> that we may reach beyond guessing to knowing,
> and beyond doubt to certainty.
> Purify our hearts,
> that wrong desires may not only be kept under control,
> but may be completely taken away.
> Strengthen our wills,
> that we may pass beyond resolving to doing,
> and beyond intention to action.

O God, our Father, this day we rest our weakness in your strength and our insufficiency in your completeness. Take us, and do for us what we cannot do, and make us what we cannot be; through Jesus Christ.

William Barclay
from Prayers for the Christian Year

Reading: Eph 4:17-32 Learn to be like Christ.

102

The feast of St. Boniface

We thank you for the zeal and energy of Saint Boniface who, in the dark ages as monk, missionary and archbishop, led the people of Germany and the Low Countries to believe in your Son Jesus Christ. Encourage us to follow his example and to tell of the gospel to those who are so concerned with the necessities of the material world that they cannot perceive their deeper needs. Help us by living our lives open to your Spirit to show the joy and wonder of life in Christ to those about us so that they, too, will want to follow him. We can so easily forget those who live and have lived heroically for you, and do not remember that with your support we may live in the same way. Give us strength and courage to spread your word of light and life in this dark world. Amen.

Reading: Heb 11:35b-12:2 They are our example.

To him be power and authority

Martin Luther King's 'last words as he left his first church at Montgomery to accept the wider leadership to which he felt history was calling him were this ascription:

"And now unto him who is able to keep us from falling and lift us from this dark valley of despair to the bright mountains of hope, from the midnight of desperation to the daybreak of joy; to him be power and authority for ever and ever. Amen"

His hope was in that power.'

Kenneth Slack
from *Martin Luther King*

Reading: Jude 24-25 To God, the only God.

Faith and trust in the face of change

You called Abraham out of his own country away from his secure life and you did not tell him where you were taking him, but he was faithful to you and followed your lead. I feel rather like him for I do not know where you are taking me. I would like to know where I stand and where I am going; and I do not like change! You seem to be telling me that I will learn true stability and happiness through constant change. Your ways are strange and you ask a lot from those who try to follow you. If ability to adapt to change and flexibility are what you want of me, give me faith and courage and a firm sense of your support. I ask this through your Son Jesus Christ. Amen.

Reading: Heb 11:8-12 The faith of Abraham and Sarah.

JUNE 8

The sin I fear

Preserve me, Lord, from the sin which I fear so much: contempt for your love. May I never sin against the Holy Spirit who is love and union, harmony and peace. May I never be separated from your Spirit, from the unity of your peace, by committing the sin which can never be forgiven, neither here nor in the world to come. Keep me, O Lord, among my brothers and kinsfolk that I may proclaim your peace. Keep me among those who preserve the unity of the Spirit in the bond of peace.

Baldwin of Canterbury (+1190)

Reading: Mt 12:24-32 Blasphemy against the Spirit will not be forgiven.

JUNE 9

Charity is death's reprieve

Be fixed and unshaken in your faith; care for each other with a brother's love, and make common cause for the truth. Give way to one another in the Lord's own spirit of courtesy, treating no one as inferior. When it is in your power to do a kindness, never put it off to another time, for charity is death's reprieve.

St. Polycarp (+c. 155)
from *Letter to the Philippians*

Reading: Rom 13:8-10 If you love your fellow men you have
carried out your obligations.

JUNE 10

Tranquility in adversity

The pollen count was high yesterday. I knew that, Lord without anyone saying it. Why? Because I sneeze. Now and then I think it would help if there were other inbuilt gauges . . . if I could feel I was about to go off the deep end in irritation or if I knew that to go to a particular place for a meeting, a party or to see a friend would put me out of control. How could that be, Lord? If I am close to you, wait on you and silently listen — will you help me to know? If I try today, give time to be still, to sit, to be open — will you fill me with wisdom? I don't know, I'm not sure, but please help me if I try?

Reading: Ps 46:8-10 Be still and know that I am God.

JUNE 11

The feast of St. Barnabas

Help me to be like Saint Barnabas who was courageous in doing your will. It must have been difficult for him to introduce Paul to the

Christians at Antioch when he had persecuted so many elsewhere, and it cannot have been easy to go on missionary journeys in those days. Help me to have courage to be loyal to you in my daily life and not to be ashamed to be known as one of your followers among people who are unbelieving and mocking. I ask this for the sake of your Son who gave his life for us.

Reading: Acts 9:22-30 The fearless preaching of Paul.

Prayer for strength to support a friend

It is not easy for us to be loyal to friends who fail us, but Saint Barnabas was. Saint Paul was exasperated with John Mark when he gave up his missionary work with him and Barnabas, and would not take him again, but Barnabas did. When friends let you, Lord, and me down, I am hurt and want to give them up. Generally it is my hurt I mind most about, and the fact that I have been made a fool of by a friend. Barnabas persisted with the cowardly Mark who through his faith in and love for your Son, became courageous enough to be a companion of Saint Paul when he was in prison, in Rome. Give me strength to support weak friends so that their faith and courage may grow as well as mine.   Amen.

Reading: Acts 15:36-41 Paul refuses to take Mark on a missionary journey.

The feast of St. Antony of Padua

A person who is filled with the Holy Spirit speaks several languages. These several languages are the various ways of witnessing to Christ, such as humility, poverty, obedience and patience, with which we speak when we practise them towards our neighbour. Language comes alive when it speaks by deeds. Enough of talking; let actions speak. We are bloated with words and empty works. That is why we are accursed by the Lord, who cursed the fig tree on which he found no fruit but only leaves. It has been laid down as a law for the preacher, says Gregory, that he should practice what he preaches. It is useless for a man to boast that he knows the law, if his behaviour contradicts his teaching.

St. Antony of Padua (+1231)
a sermon.

Reading: Mk 11:12-19. Christ the fig tree and the Temple.

The feast of St. Basil

Saint Basil defended the poor and downtrodden and was brave in standing up to those who queried his beliefs in an age when Christian doctrines were being formulated; though he was wise in so many ways, first as a good monk, and then as a bishop who carefully tended his flock, he was often tactless and headstrong. I so often get discouraged by the perfection of the saints; they appear so unlike us who seem to fail you so many times, but Basil had this sense of failure too. Give me strength to continue to follow you even when I have sinned and feel hopeless. Help me to get up and ask for forgiveness, and continue to bear with myself knowing that you, in your love, accept me as I am and will heal my wounds and strengthen my feeble steps.   Amen.

Reading: Rm 7:18-25 St. Paul's sense of wretchedness

JUNE 15

Guide the vessel of our life

O Lord our God, teach us, to ask thee aright for the right blessings. Guide the vessel of our life toward thyself, thou tranquil haven of all storm-tossed souls. Show us the course wherein we should go. Renew a willing spirit within us. Let thy Spirit curb our wayward senses, and guide and enable us, unto that which is our true good, to keep thy laws and in all our works evermore to rejoice in thy glories and gladdening presence. For thine is the glory and praise of all thy saints for ever and ever.

St. Basil (*c.* 330-379)

Reading: 1 Pet 3:18-22 Christ died to lead us to God.

JUNE 16

The value of the Psalms

The psalm soothes anger, frees from care and drives away sadness. It is a weapon by night and a teacher by day; it is a shield in times of fear, an occasion of rejoicing for the holy, a mirror of tranquility; it is a pledge of peace and harmony, for with the aid of the harp the psalm makes one melody from a number of different notes. The beginning of the day hears the sound of the psalm and the end of the day its echoes.

St. Ambrose (*c.* 340-397)
from his *Commentary on the Psalms*

Reading: Eph 5:19-20 Sing the words and tunes of the psalms.

God's word is a living thing

Saint Paul exclaims:
'God's word is a living thing!'
Living — that means —
    It's actual,
being spoken at this very moment,
continually and tirelessly repeated,
born in God's heart every day to be
transmitted to living men,
and it's always fresh,
new for each and every man,
Personal,
meant to illuminate him individually.
This word's 'the true light that enlightens
everyone who comes into the world.'
There's not a soul on earth God doesn't speak to.

Louis Evely
from *That Man is You*

Reading: Heb 4:12-13 It cuts like a double-edged sword.

Father-Mother God

Jesus, you taught us that God is our Father. Today, I want to sit a moment and think what 'Father' means. My experience of Father is my own, and it is kindly, vague and distant, because I hardly knew him before he died. Another person knows Father as a loving friendly person growing to be a brother. Yet another has a fearful picture of a tyrant who bullies and beats and is to be avoided. Perhaps, Jesus, you were biased when you told us to call God our Father. He is Mother also, and basically he is LOVE.

Loving Father-Mother God. Let us know your love.

Reading: 1 Jn 4:9-11 God's love for us was revealed
              when God sent unto the world his only Son.

The feast of St. Romuald

Saint Romuald chose to live alone; he had the courage to do so. Today so many live in cities on their own; they have no choice. Saint Romuald found you in his aloneness, discovered the wonder of you in prayer and in creation, and he taught others this way of life. Teach me, teach all the lonely, how to find you when we are on our own. Speak to us through the Bible, through creation, through music, through silence and open our ears to hear and our eyes to see. Be with us in our hearts and then, Lord, in our aloneness, we will not be lonely.

Reading: Lk 6:12 He spent the whole night in prayer.

JUNE 20

The feast of St. Alban

I thank you, Lord, for Saint Alban, the first Christian martyr in England. Give me the kind of bravery he showed when he sheltered a Christian fleeing from death, and then laid down his life courageously for you. I so often let you down by failing to defend Christian standards and beliefs when others mock them. It does not seem worthwhile supporting them openly when the people take no notice of what I say and laugh at me. Give me the right words and the courage to say them.

Reading: 1 Pet 1:3-9 Plagued by all sorts of trials.

JUNE 21

Prayer for those under persecution

Lord, help me to pray for those who are being persecuted for their faith, those who are being imprisoned and put to death and those who are deprived of their rights as human beings because they follow Jesus, your Son. I so often forget them and only pray about my own little troubles, and anxieties. Support and strengthen the persecuted so that they do not deny what they believe to be right; convert those who injure them so they may repent of the evil which they do.   Amen.

Reading: 1 Thess 1:2-6 We always mention you in your prayers.

JUNE 22

The feast of St. Thomas More

We have been ordained by God to this end; to follow nature is to conform to the dictates of reason on what we seek and avoid.

The first dictate of reason is ardently to love and revere the divine majesty, to whom we owe what we are and whatever happiness we can reach.

Secondly, reason warns us and summons us to lead our lives as calmly and as cheerfully as we can, and to help others to attain to this goal.

St. Thomas More (1478-1535)

Reading: Prov 15:13-15 Cheerfulness.

Grant me clear confidence that you exist

How easy it is for me to live with you, Lord!
How easy it is for me to believe in you!
When my mind is distraught and my reason fails,
When the cleverest people do not see further than this evening what must
    be done tomorrow
You grant me the clear confidence that you exist, and that you will take
    care
that not all the ways of goodness are stopped.
At the height of earthly fame I gaze with wonder at that path through
    hopelessness -
to this point from which even I have been able
to convey to men some reflection of the Light which comes from you.
And you will enable me to go on doing
as much as needs to be done.
And in so far as I do not manage it —
that means you have allotted the task to others.

Alexander Solzhenitsyn

Reading: 2 Thess 2:13-17 & 3:1-5 May the Lord comfort and strengthen you.

The birthday of John the Baptist

Help me to prepare a way for you to enter
    more deeply into my heart;
Help me to see the things in my heart which stop
    your coming;
Help me to repent of my sins which get in the
    way of your coming;
Without your light shining in my heart, I cannot
    see what is getting in your way;
Without the strength you give I will not be able to
    clear a way for you;
Without your love and understanding I will not be
    able to accept your forgiveness.
But with your light, your strength and your love in my heart
    I will be able to show forth your glory in the world.

Reading: Lk 7:18-30 Christ testifies to John.

Give me the right words

John the Baptist came to prepare the way for your Son and he bravely preached the need for repentance. Show me, Lord, how to preach the good news of your Son in a bewildered world which does not seem to know how to repent or what they should repent of! How do I prepare the way for your Son to come into the lives of people who do not sense their need of his love and message of your forgiveness? I know that your Spirit is with me; help me to be a channel through which he comes to reveal you to those who recognise they have needs and require healing. Give me an open, brave heart and the right words at the right times.

Reading: Lk 1:76-79 A voice cries in the wilderness.

Thanksgiving for those who preach Christ

Thank you, O God, for the courage and faith of all those men and women who, from the time of the apostles, preached the gospel of the living Christ; those who were strong in the face of persecution; those who brought the good news to this land of ours; and for those, who, in recent years, have gone out to teach and preach in the name of Christ their Lord.

Be with your church in every land. Strengthen her when she is weak, encourage her when she is failing, give her humility where she is proud, and self-confident; and where, day by day, she is seeking to show others the joy of your kingdom, deepen her faith in her risen Lord.

Help us to realize that we are part of your great church universal and that together with all your children we can worship and adore, through Jesus Christ our Lord.

From *Prayers for Today's Church* (1972)

Reading: Eph 1:15-23 The triumph and supremacy of Christ.

Undefeated

He said not: Thou shalt not be tempted, thou shalt not be travailed, thou shalt not be afflicted; but he said: Thou shalt not be overcome.

Lady Julian of Norwich (1342-c. 1412)

Reading: Jer 1:4-19 The Lord is with you to deliver you.

The comfort in the failures of St. Peter

Thank you for Saint Peter; he is a great comfort to me. I do so many things wrong and so often fail in what I try to do that I start to worry.

Then I remember Saint Peter who denied you three times and who though he realized that you were the Christ, thought he knew better than you how to set about saving the world, yet you used him in the founding of your church.

Stop me from dwelling on my failures and show me how to learn from them. Use me, faults and all to work for you in daily life as you used Saint Peter.

Reading: Mk 8:27-33 Faith and faithlessness in Peter.

The feast of St. Peter

We praise you, Lord Christ, for your apostle Simon Peter, the man of rock:

For his bold confession of your name;
For his courageous leadership of the apostolic church;
For his abounding zeal in your service;
For his love and loyalty to you, his Lord.

Give us the same rock-like qualities of faith, courage and devotion in your service, and keep us steadfast to the end, for the honour of your great name.

Frank Colquhoun
from *Contemporary Parish Prayers* (1975)
Reading: Mt 16:13-20 Simon, you are a happy man.

Commemoration of St. Paul

Saint Paul was enormously brave physically and the pains and hardships he suffered for you amaze us and sometimes daunt us when we think of our own lack of courage. To be brave seems to have come naturally to him; you created him this way! For him, I think, Lord, the greatest martyrdom was to be patient with the failings of others; he got really angry with Christians who failed to live up to the high standard of self-giving which he, through your grace, had achieved. He was annoyed with the clever Corinthians and the foolish Galatians, and he probably was rougher with them than he should have been because he found patience difficult. Is it because of his realization of this weakness that he is able to write so tellingly of Christian love which should keep on being respectful, kind and understanding of others?

Give us your gift of love so that we may persist in being patient with ourselves and others however difficult and trying this may be. We ask this through Jesus Christ, your Son and our example.

Reading: 2 Cor 12:11-15 Because I love you more.

111

July

Doubt helped by prayer
The example of Saint Benedict
Our own inadequacy and sinfulness, seen in Saint Mary Magdalen and leading to repentance and self-giving

In the British Isles, July heralds a time when many young people in school and university have done what they can in examinations, and now face both the results and the world. This gives an atmosphere of self-doubt, rootlessness, a fear of inadequacy and sometimes even despair. Other regions of the world may react differently, because their seasons are different, which will be a good thought for us about the diversity of God's creation.

We must not sink down in self-pity or even self-aggrandizement. It is for us as Christians to try to look straight at ourselves and the world, to make an assessment and to keep going ahead in the love and service of God and of each other.

Because we are inextricably bound together as human beings, the pattern of our sorrow, doubt, prayer, repentance and acceptance of God's mercy and love will, in fact, have a feed-back upon our neighbours and the world in general.

Starting July, then, with questioning and doubt, we have the great example of Saint Thomas. If we are boosted by his sudden realisation as expressed in his saying, 'My Lord and My God', then we, too, must react. There is every reason why we should express our doubt and difficulty to God because, as our loving Father, he understands and sympathises. But he is God, God of infinite wisdom and personal touch. He will lead us — and we must be confident of this. Thomas, once converted to deep belief, in the short time before his martyrdom is traditionally associated with work in India. This widens our horizons.

We are widened in a different way as we approach the feast of Saint

Benedict, Father of Western Monasticism. Here the fleeing from the world reacted into a worldwide calling of *followers to live the Gospel.* It must be true that not every priest, sister or fellow Christian has responded to the call day by day and indeed we can swing from praise and joy in the universe to self-doubt.

So it is good this month to focus upon the feast of Saint Mary Magdalen and to be able to accept her as an example of wilfulness and then total surrender to God. Through sadness, sorrow and repentance we have a chance for the rest of the month to review our own personal response, our sense of justice and the breadth of our self-giving in love both of God and our neighbour.

A prayer for calmness and control

Grant calmness and control of thought to those who are facing uncertainty and anxiety; let their heart stand fast, believing in the Lord. Be thou all things to all men, knowing each one and his petition, each house and its need, for the sake of Jesus Christ.   Amen.

Russian Liturgy

Reading: Mt 8:23-27 Jesus calms the sea

Is there God?

The fool has said in his heart, 'There is no God' . . . so says the Psalm. But, Lord God, today there are men and women whom the world calls wise, intellectual, leaders of thought, and many of them say there is no God. It is very hard for those of us who believe and constantly meet this denial, or just the complete indifference of so many. Why do you seem irrelevant if you do exist, Lord? Is this what faith really means that I should say: 'Lord I believe. Please help my unbelief'?

Reading: Ps 14 The fool has said in his heart.

The feast of St. Thomas, apostle

Lord, you comfort me greatly when I am in difficulty and doubt, because you have yourself chosen Thomas to be your close follower during your life on earth. And he doubted, Lord, until the wonderful moment when he gave himself utterly to you in his heartfelt: 'My Lord and my God.' Help all of us further, Lord, by his example to grow from doubt to faith, that like him we may go wherever your Spirit calls us to preach the Good News of your love and patience. Especially today the great sub-continent of India comes to mind in prayer, since tradition tells of Thomas' journey to India. There are so many millions who still cannot hear your word of love to them. Give them faith as you did to Thomas that they too may say: 'My Lord and my God.'

Reading: Jn 20:24-29 Unless I see, I refuse to believe.

115

For the insight to see my priorities

When I look at the world today I think we must have lost our saltiness, our savour. We, who say we are your Son's followers, do not seem to have much influence or know what we should be doing. Perhaps we have let the world drain off that special saltiness that you gave your first disciples. Do we give up too easily? It is so hard to influence the trend away from you and so easy to grow into a mushy kind of pious materialism!

Help me Lord, to forget myself, the image I have made of you for myself, the image which my group gives you, and all images and ideals which come between you and me. Help me to respond to the leadings of your Spirit so that I may learn your will and come to experience Christ, your Son, alive with and in me. I will have to give things up, but I trust that you will give me a clear sense of right and wrong which will stop me from getting caught into today's colourless indifference. Lord, make me courageous enough to be your salt in this insipid world!

Reading: Lk 14:28-35 Salt is a useful thing.

JULY 5

For insight and strength to make the right choice

Lord, sometimes I feel myself pulled in different directions. Part of me feels I should stand up and assert myself, state my position, make sure that I am understood and that people accept me for what I am. Part of me says to myself that I am stupid, proud and presumptious: I should really just relax and let things happen as God wills them. But what do you want of me Lord? Am I to stand on my own feet and be a full person? Or am I to submit myself to be trodden upon? I find it difficult to understand what you do want, Lord. Can you help me to listen and understand and then to be the right person, to do the right thing . . . according to your will?

Reading: Jn 15:1-8 Cut off from me you can do nothing.

JULY 6

Why?

Lord, again and again, I ask you 'Why?' when I see the injustice that takes place in the world; so many innocent people die through lack of food, through persecution or through neglect. Why, do you do nothing to stop man's inhumanity to his brothers and sisters? Have you forsaken us? I try to trust you and to believe that you care for us like a tender Father, but so much in life today makes me doubt. I cannot stop questioning you but beg you to help my unbelief and not to leave me comfortless!

Reading: Job 24:1-25 A lament of Job.

My prayer rises like incense

The whole of the spiritual life turns on these two things: we are troubled when we contemplate ourselves and our sorrow brings salvation; when we contemplate God we are restored so that we receive consolation from the joy of the Holy Spirit. From the contemplation of ourselves we gain fear and humility; but from the contemplation of God, hope and love.

St. Bernard (1090-1153)
from a *Sermon*

Reading: Ps 4 Lord, I am calling.

A prayer of humble obedience

I think a lot of my difficulty with day by day life, Lord, is in my wanting to know all the answers, to see the justice in what is happening, and to grasp what I must do. Instead of being humble under your gentle hand, pride rules my thoughts and actions. In praying for some humility today, I am asking to have the strong simplicity of Saint Benedict in obediently following your call to the desert, even when it may take a long time to get rid of the trappings of the world. You, Jesus, always searched for the will of your Father; so did Benedict. May I have the patience, humility and love to do the same. Amen.

Reading: Mk 10:13-16 Welcoming the kingdom of God like a little child.

A prayer for peace of mind and heart

Saint Benedict fled from the riches and squalour of Rome to a cave in the hills, Lord, so that he might find you in solitude and peace. And he did, Lord, for which we thank you, because of what we owe to Saint Benedict through your inspiration. But now, in the hustle and degradation of today's world, please instil into our minds and hearts that peace which the world does not give. Let your peace flow like a river over the dry aridity of our souls, until with calm tranquility we can be ourselves at peace, and so become channels of your peace to others.

Reading: Ezek 47:1-12 The spring in the temple.

A prayer for perception

O gracious and holy Father, give us
Wisdom to perceive thee;
Intelligence to understand thee;

117

Diligence to seek thee;
Patience to wait for thee;
Eyes to behold thee;
A heart to meditate upon thee;
And a life to proclaim thee:
through the power of the Spirit of
Jesus Christ our Lord.

St. Benedict (*c*.480-c. 547)

Reading: Wis 6:12-20 Finding wisdom
    or Prov 8:1-22.

JULY 11

The feast of St. Benedict

Lord, teach me how to meditate and how to contemplate. Give me that stillness of prayer which will allow me to be completely open to your word and your love. Search me through with your Spirit that like Saint Benedict whose feast we keep today, I may grow ever deeper in knowledge of your way and so come with joy and peace through a calm life to a happy death.

Reading: Is 52:7-12 How beautiful on the mountains.

JULY 12

For conservation of God's world

In the way your world has developed and the big cities and urban districts have evolved, there is so much room for poverty and misery, Lord. How is it that the brilliant achievements of human minds get bleared and filthy in working the raw materials of need and comfort? You, Jesus Christ, experienced toil as a carpenter and the poverty of the countryside. May you lead the planners to humanise your surroundings and industrialists, unions and workers to join together in bettering conditions.

Reading: Mt 13:24-30 Wheat and weeds growing together.

JULY 13

On the value of reading the Psalms

Whoever reads the Psalms finds a special remedy to cure the wounds caused by his own passions. Whoever is at pains to read the Psalms will find in them a sort of gymnasium for the use of all souls, a sort of stadium of virtue, where different sorts of exercises are set out before him, from which he can choose the best suited to train him to win his crown.

St. Ambrose (*c*.340-397)
from his *Commentary on the Psalms*

Reading: Ps 119 Happy those who walk in the Law of the Lord.

Quietness and modesty in prayer

When we pray, our words and petitions must be properly ordered. They must have quietness and modesty in them. Let us consider that we are standing in the sight of God, to whom our bodily attitude and tone of voice must be pleasant . . . the modest man should pray quietly . . . The Lord himself instructed us to pray in secret, in hidden and remote places, even in our own bedrooms.

St. Cyprian (c.200-258)
from *On the Lord's Prayer*

Reading: Mt 6:5-6 When you pray . . .

The feast of St. Bonaventure

. . . 'We can do nothing unless divine aid supports us. This divine aid is at hand for all who seek it with truly humble and devout heart. To seek thus is to sigh for divine aid in fervent prayer. Prayer then is the mother and origin of every upward striving of the soul. Thus Dionysius, in his book, *Mystical Theology,* wishing to instruct us in the transports of the soul, opens first with a prayer. Let us, therefore, pray and say to the Lord, our God: 'Conduct me, O Lord, in thy way and I will enter thy truth: let my heart rejoice that it may fear thy name.'

St. Bonaventure (1221-1274)
from *Itinerarium mentis in Deo*

Reading: Ps 83:6-12 Blessed is the man who trusts in you.

A cosmic hymn of praise

O God of mountains, stars and boundless space!
O God of Freedom and of joyous hearts!
When Thy Face looketh forth from all men's faces,
There will be room enough in crowded marts;
Brood Thou around me, and the noise is o'er;
Thy universe my closet with shut door.

George MacDonald (1824-1905)

Reading: Ps 148 Alleluia! Praise the Lord!

The humility of the rich

It is certain that the poor more easily achieve the blessing of humility than the rich. Gentleness goes with poverty, pride more commonly with riches. And yet, very many rich people do use their wealth for works of

119

charity rather than as a means to puff their pride. This spirit counts as among its greatest profits what it spends in relieving distress and hardship in others.

St. Leo the Great (+461)

Reading: Lk 19:1-10 Story of Zeccheus.

JULY 18

Loose me, Lord

O Lord,
>   I am Lazarus
>   bound with the grave clothes
>   of habits and fears,
>   struggling towards the light
>   through the opening
>   of the rolled away stone,
>   answering thy command —
>   'Lazarus come forth!'
>   awaiting the second command —
>   'Loose him and let him go.'
>   Loose me from habits and fears,
>   the dead hand of the past,
>   into new freedom, new life,
>   ready to obey
>   thy further commands.

George Appleton
from The Word is the Seed

Reading: Jn 11:43-44 Lazarus is loosed from the grave clothes.

JULY 19

Feeling loved but unworthy

When I feel your love, Lord, it is sometimes very hard. You see, I feel such a useless, hopeless burden on you. One minute I say I'll give you everything . . . the next I seem to take it back. Now I am quite happy to do what I want, right or wrong. Later I am full of a sense of sin, failure, letting you down. What a terrible mix-up I am, so that I often think I do not even know right from wrong. Paul once wrote: 'Who will rid me? . . .' this I can echo. And it is worse when I *know* you love me so much. I can only say now how much it means that you love me; how much it means that I still love myself more than I love you. Help me to love as I am loved, unworthy as I am of your great love.

Reading: 1 Cor 15:54-58 Victory through our Lord Jesus Christ.

Sorrow for sin

The people of the world today, including myself, so often get blurred on what sin is, Lord. I suppose partly it is because we are not very clear about who you are, because after all sin is not a thing, but a hurtful break in relationship between me and you, between me and my neighbour. But I always have so many excuses for myself. There are so many reasons why my attitude is right for me, my temper had to be lost, there was no sin in such-and-such. I'm sure I kid myself an awful lot, and so I want to ask you that I may have some of that sorrow that Mary Magdalen had, a sorrow growing into a joyful love. I, too, would like to come through your forgiveness and your friendship to stand beside your cross and share in your pain, that knowing your love for me, I may share that love with others till they are both filled with sorrow and filled with love.

Reading: Mk 15:40-47 & 16:1-11 Christ and Mary of Magdala.

The hardness of being alone

Sometimes a great loneliness comes over my mind and heart, Lord. Much as I love, much as I know I am loved, I am still an individual and alone. At times like these, and always if possible, give me, Jesus, an assurance of your presence, the comfort of your love. Yet, I know I must not be greedy or expect a wrong expression of your love. You need to seem absent from me as well as present, if I am to grow. I understand this, Lord . . . but O, it is so hard to be alone.

Reading: Jn 6:60-71 Will you too go away?

The feast of St. Mary Magdalen

Dear God, so often I feel with Mary Magdalen that 'they have taken away my Lord and I do not know where they have laid him'. I do not know where you are or what you look like. I realize that you appear differently to us at different times and that we must never cling to the form you showed us last. Sometimes too, you reveal yourself by being absent; then we know the picture, the experience we had of you was too small and too limited, yet we want to keep it. When you leave us in ageless and lost we realize how much we need you and then we come to see how close you are to us even in darkness. Help me never to cling to past visions but to follow your lead however obscure the way may be, trusting that your Holy Spirit will always guide me when I feel lost.

Reading: Jn 20:11-18 Mary Magdalen and Jesus after the Resurrection.

Cast out evil from our hearts

Most merciful Father, whose compassion was revealed to Mary Magdalen in transforming power: cast out from our hearts all that is evil and make us new in Christ; and grant us such gratitude for your love that we, like her, may minister to the needs of your people and be witnesses to our risen Lord. In his name we ask it.

Llewllyn Cummings
from *Contemporary Parish Prayers*

Reading: Lk 8:1-3 The women accompanying Jesus.

Forgive me as you forgave Magdalen

When I fail you in shameful ways, which I often try to hide from myself, I think of Mary Magdalen and marvel how your Son forgave and loved her. O God, is your goodness and love so great that you take back into your care people like me who keep on falling? Teach me how to accept and truly believe that you love me as I am now spots, wrinkles and all. Guide me so that I become what you would like me to be. I ask this through Jesus Christ. Amen.

Reading: 1 Tim 1:15-17 Christ came into the world to save sinners.

The feast of St. James

In celebrating the feast of Saint James we are brought very close to you, Lord Jesus, because you chose out James and Peter and John for certain intimate revelations like the Transfiguration and the Agony in the Garden. We thank you for the example you give us in him and especially for his acceptance of the ultimate way of offering his life for you in his martyrdom. We understand that his zeal for the proclaiming of the Good News was such that a quick martyrdom was inevitable. And so on his day we ask that we are strong, courageous and filled with zeal to spread your word, whatever this may cost in humiliation, rebuff and loss of friends.

Reading: Mt 20:20-21 The sons of Zebedee.

Money is a problem

It is said that money is the root of all evil. On the other hand, today it may be said that without money, penniless, you are lost. Sit for a few minutes today and think in your own mind what money means to you. Are you 'all right'? That is satisfied and not bothering? Have you got too much, so that you could not care less about money or people's worry? At the other end, do you find it hard to know where money will come from for the next meal? (If so I wonder how you can afford to read this book?) Would it be good to sit and think quite simply about what money means to YOU?

Reading: Lk 21-1-4 The story of the widow's mite.

JULY 27

How is my conscience about justice?

'If the Lord does not build the house, in vain do the builders labour.' So much time in this world is spent in building . . . our houses, our roads, our factories, our dreams. How often, Lord, are you involved in this building. Do governments really build for the people or for their own political career? Do business men and women think of the poor and the under-privileged or of their own enrichment? Do workers work for others or for themselves? I know, Lord, that I often forget that without you I can do nothing. I often think I can build the house.

Reading: Mt 7:21-27 The sensible man builds his house on rock.

JULY 28

The pattern of true holy living

Let this, brethren, be the pattern of your life, of true holy living:

Dwell with Christ in that eternal homeland in both your thought and yearning.

Turn away from no service of love for Christ in this troubled pilgrimage.

Ascend to the Father by following the Lord Christ heavenward to become free, whole and alive in leisurely meditation.

Return to your brother by following Christ earthward to be torn and divided into a thousand pieces, to become all things to all men in good works.

Disdain nothing that comes from Christ, value nothing which is not for Christ.

Thirst for one thing, have but one concern where Christ is one.

Serve the many brothers in whom Christ lives manifold.

Isaac of Stella (+1169)

Reading: Jas 1:19-27 Listen to the word, and obey.

JULY 29

For justice in the economy

In Genesis, the future of mankind is laid down starkly . . . toil, sweat and

123

pain. Today there is a big division of 'the haves' and the 'have-nots'. In so many countries there is no work for some, because they do not need to work; for others there is just no work . . . unemployment. In many ways these are equally degrading ways of life, Lord, though the second is more painful and obvious. Help us to get our economy on better lines, with more thought for the underdog, more fairness in the use of the world's materials, greater concern to make sure every single human person can live a human life.

Reading: Jas 4:13-17 & 5:1-6 A warning on justice.

JULY 30

Love everyone, your brother

When on a particular occasion I meet someone or a group of people who seem useless, good-for-nothing-lay-abouts. I find it very easy to sneer at them, despise them, write them off. It is not only that there is much to criticise in myself, Lord, but it is also my failure to understand the love you have for every tiniest piece of your creation, and especially your everlasting love for human beings, rich and poor, clever and dull, good and bad. Give me eyes to see with your eyes, Lord Jesus.

Reading: Mt 18:1-14 Who is the greatest?

JULY 31

The feast of St. Ignatius of Loyola

Take, Lord, all my liberty. Receive my memory, my understanding and my whole will. Whatever I have and possess Thou has given to me; to thee I restore it wholly, and to thy will I utterly surrender it for thy direction. Give me the love of thee only, with thy grace, and I am rich enough; nor ask I anything beside.

St. Ignatius of Loyola (1491-1556)

Reading: Gal 2:20-21 I live with the life of Christ.

August

Praise and glory
Relaxation to enjoy God and nature
A holiday

As we are writing in England, in the European zone of the northern hemisphere, we are inclined to associate August with a holiday season and part of such warm summer as we get. For others, we forget, this is a season of winter when school is in session and not on vacation, when the bulk of work may well be done before the hot weather begins and the local people make their holiday plans.

So be it. This can emphasise the variety of the world of God, and i is best for us to live in our own situation. We are therefore looking t August as a fruitful time, a time when perhaps the family can relax together, away from the immediacy of work for the parents and school for the children. It is a time when more and more people are finding it possible to go out from a city or urban situation into the country, to be beside the sea or even to go from their own country to visit some other as tourists.

It may then be appropriate for anyone who wishes a guide to prayer at this time to rest a little in the Lord, to take a gentle look round about in order to appreciate more the blossoming and fruiting of God's world in which we live so that its impression upon us may call up from our hearts a burst of praise to the glory of God.

Such a burst is helped early on in the month by concentrating on the celebration of the Transfiguration of Christ, which made so deep an impression on Peter and the other two disciples — but which led to the direct command from the Father in heaven: 'Listen to him'. In this period we could well accept that command wherever we may be and seek to be still and open before the glory of God in nature, in his saints, in the possibility of our own transfiguration. Not one of us should look at a grain of wheat without realising how it will be transfigured into fields almost ready for the harvest; or look at the abundance of lettuce, cabbage, beans, tomatoes, marigolds, stock, and all the other flower, vegetable and cereal crops, which only a few short months ago were apparently dead seeds. Dare we look at all this and then say that God could not transfigure us by the sun of his love just as he has transfigured the seeds of the earth?

In a practical way, even though timing may be difficult, see that some period of quiet, of silence, of being alone and out in the open can be hugely valuable to your peace of mind, your depth and the amount you have to give to the family, to friends, to neighbours, to the church, or to your daily work. If it is possible to have some 'input' not simply by relaxing but by reading, listening to a tape of music or instruction, of just getting together with one or two others, see if you can manage it. Often such a thing seems impossible and hardly worth the effort. Try it . . . and you will know the value.

Lammas: The beginning of the harvest

O God, who hast made heaven and earth and all that is in them: we humbly ask thee to bless and hallow these first fruits of corn, and to multiply them abundantly for us who offer them; and grant such seasonable weather that this year's harvest may be plentiful, and we, rejoicing in thy gifts, may pay our thanks to thy divine majesty; through Jesus Christ our Lord.

Country Services

Reading: Ps 65 The Lord gives us the increase.

God's creation in a rose

I take a rose and look at it. The petals curl, the heart is full and soft and radiant, but somehow self-contained. Deep yellow becomes lighter and then at the petal's edge turns crimson. The beauty of what you have made helps me to sit still and look, listening to your presence in the loveliness of nature, glimpsing your variety in the differing roses, trying to grasp the hardness of the thorn, the lush green of the leaves, the strength and channelled goodness of the stem. When will I learn the impossibility of coming to the end of wonder at your varied beauty, Lord?

Reading: Song 2:8-17 The flowers appear on the earth.

Seeing God in nature

There is a vision of you;
the world of creation
reflects it in its beauty,
in the mountains, the
sky, the sea, the variety
of greenness in the trees,
in the rose, in the daisy
in the shininess of an apple.
In so many ways you
show yourself to us.
But most real to me

127

is your closeness,
your hidden nearness.
How can I share
this awareness, this
vision which transforms
all things? Show me,
I beg you, how to
do this, dear Lord!

Reading: Ps 103 God's love lasts from all eternity.

AUGUST 4

The feast of St. John Vianney, Curé d'Ars

Man has a noble task: that of prayer and love. To pray and to love, that is the happiness of man on earth.

Prayer is nothing else than union with God. When the heart is pure and united with God it is consoled and filled with sweetness; it is dazzled by a marvellous light. In this initimate union God and the soul are like two pieces of wax moulded into one; they cannot any more be separated. It is a very wonderful thing, this union of God with his insignificant creature, a happiness passing all understanding.

St. John Vianney (1786-1859)
from one of his *Instructions*

Reading: 1 Pet 2:4-10 He called out of darkness.

AUGUST 5

The Transfiguration of Christ

I love the story of Jesus' transfiguration; how the disciples saw him shining and glorious, and his glory surely touched the hillside around him and transformed all nature too. In the summer when the sun lights the sea and the hillsides, I remember the glory and beauty of your Son and I try to let it touch my life and change me. But I find that I do not really want to be changed and trans-figured. The cost of transfiguration is great; it means nothing less than the losing of myself, the handing over of myself to you. It is a frightening thing to do and I do not know what will happen next. After your Son's transfiguration, came the journey to Jerusalem and death on a cross. Lord, give me courage and love enough to let you transform and transfigure me!

Reading: Mt 17:1-8 The story of the transfiguration.

The feast of the Transfiguration of Christ
On the mountain when you were transfigured, the disciples had a vision of your glory. They must have seen something of it in your daily life but perhaps their eyes had not been open. We, too, Lord Jesus Christ, accepting you as our friend and our support, often forget or fail to see that you are the king of glory. We think we understand what you said and did, and do not perceive how deep and mysterious you and your words are. We are so trivial and see you only superficially, forgetting that you are the way that leads to God, your Almighty and glorious Father. Friend and brother, Lord and Master, we adore you and thank you for showing us your glory.   Amen.
Reading: Mk 9:2-8 The Transfiguration.

The Transfiguration
I thank you for revealing something of your glory to your Son's disciples when he was speaking with Moses and Elijah, prophets who both had experienced the mystery of your closeness and aloofness. Moses was aware of your glory and majesty on the mountain, and Elijah knew your nearness and that you speak to us in gentleness and love with a still, small, voice. Your Son's three disciples were bewildered and overwhelmed by his glory on the mount of transfiguration, I, too, cannot comprehend this dazzling revelation. Clear my eyes so that they may see, make my ears alert to your gentle voice, and give me an understanding heart so that I will be able to come down from the mountain of glory to help the wounded and bruised of the world who have had no vision.
Reading: Lk 9:28-36 The Transfiguration.

The feast of St. Dominic
Dominic's frequent and special prayer for himself was to beg from God true and efficacious charity for the salvation of men, for he was convinced that just as our Saviour, the Lord Jesus, gave himself totally for our salvation, only when he, Dominic, had devoted himself to the winning of souls would he truly be a member of Christ. When he had pondered the matter long and deeply he founded the Order of Friars Preachers for this very purpose.
He often exhorted the friars, both in his writings and by his words, to

study the sacred scriptures, in the old and new testaments. He always carried a copy of the gospel according to Saint Matthew and the epistles of Saint Paul; these he had studied to such an extent that he almost knew them by heart.

From Selected Sources of the History of the Order of Preachers

Reading: Mt 10:24-33 The disciple should grow like his master.

AUGUST 9

Transfigure me, Lord

Lord, we know that we are incompetent to heal ourselves, to sanctify ourselves, to transfigure ourselves. Our holiness is your action in us, through our willingness to accept the indwelling of your Spirit. Heal me, Lord. Sanctify me, Lord. Transfigure me, Lord. Fill me, Lord. Direct me, Lord, Use me, Lord.

George Appleton
from Journey of a Soul

Reading: 2 Pet 1:16-18 Peter's account of what he saw.

AUGUST 10

Unfaltering praise of mine

Lord, be it thine,
Unfaltering praise of mine!
To thee my whole heart's love be given
Of earth and Heaven Thou King Divine!
Lord, be it thine,
Unfaltering praise of mine!
And, O pure prince! make clear my way
To serve and pray at thy sole shrine!
Lord, be it thine,
Unfaltering praise of mine!
O father of all souls that long,
Take this my song and make it thine!

Translated from the Irish
by Robin Flower (+1946)

Reading: Ps 138 In praise of the Lord.

AUGUST 11

The feast of St. Clare, foundress of the Poor Clares,
friend of St. Francis

We rejoice in Saint Clare who was so close to Saint Francis and understood him so well that she has been able to transmit his message to others down the ages. She teaches us something of the lowliness and humility of your Son by her love for his humble birth and shameful death on the cross: she shows us how by deep contemplative prayer we can support each other if we give ourselves in complete trust to you. Give us the kind of joyous love and intuition Saint Clare had so that we, by our prayer, may strengthen each other and go about preaching the gospel of Jesus Christ, crucified and risen. Amen.

Reading: Phil 2:5-11 Have this mind among yourselves which was in Christ Jesus.

AUGUST 12

Glory be to you, Lord

Glory be to you, Lord, for apples and eggs.
Glory be to you, Lord, for bicycles and babies.
Glory be to you, Lord, for mothers and houses.
Glory be to you, Lord, for dogs and leaves on trees.
Glory be to you, Lord, for stars and puddles that reflect them.
Glory be to you, Lord, for bread which feeds and grapes for wine.
Glory be to you, Lord, for man and for woman, life and death.
Glory be to you, Lord, for sleep and rest, energy and joy.
Glory be to you, Lord, for Jesus Christ, God-man, beloved.
Glory, glory, glory, glory, glory be to you, Lord. Amen.

Reading: Gen 1:11-12 God saw that it was good.

AUGUST 13

Giving you great glory

Justify my soul, O God, but also from your fountains fill my will with fire . . . Let my eyes see nothing in the world but your glory, and let my hands touch nothing that is not for your service . . . let me use all things for one sole reason; to find my joy in giving You great glory.

Thomas Merton (1915-1968)

Reading: Ps 24 Praising the king of glory.

AUGUST 14

Give me words to tell of you

You are neither darkness nor light; you are the contrast between them! You are between the darkness and light; you are greater than either. You let me know this in a way that escapes knowing. O wonderful Lord, give me words to tell of you and words to give thanks for this indescribable knowledge. Let all the world be caught into this indescribable joy.

Reading: Ex 24:15-18 & Ps 72:18-19 May the whole world be filled with his glory.

The Falling asleep or Assumption of Mary the Virgin

If I have understood
She holds high motherhood
Towards all our ghostly good
And plays in grace her part
About man's beating heart,
Laying, like air's fine flood,
the deathdance in his blood;
Yet no part but what will
Be Christ our Saviour still.
Of her flesh he took flesh:
He does take fresh and fresh,
Though much the mystery how,
Not flesh but spirit now
And makes, O marvellous!
New Nazareths in us,
Where she shall yet conceive
Him morning, noon, and eve;
New Bethlems, and he born
There, evening, noon, and morn —
Bethlem or Nazareth,
Men here may draw like breath
More Christ and baffle death;
Who, born so, comes to be
New self and nobler me
In each one and each one
More makes, when all is done,
Both God's and Mary's Son.

Gerard Manley Hopkins (1844-1889)
from *The Blessed Virgin Compared to the Air We Breathe*
Reading: Lk 1:42-45 Visitation and Magnificat.

Where shall I find you, Lord?

Lord, where shall I find You?
High and hidden is your place.
And where shall I not find you?
The world is full of Your glory.

I have sought Your nearness,
With all my heart I called You

and in going out to meet You
I found You coming in to meet me.

Judah Halevi (*c.*1075-1141)
from *Forms of Prayer for Jewish Worship*

Reading: Ps 113 Enthroned on high, he needs to stoop.

Delight in simple things

O God, who has made the heaven and the earth and all that is good and lovely therein, and hast shown us through Jesus Christ our Lord that the secret of joy is a heart free from selfish desires, help us to find delight in simple things, and ever to rejoice in the riches of thy bounty, through Jesus Christ our Lord.

From *The Kingdom, Power and the Glory*

Reading: Col 3:1-4 Your life is hid with Christ in God.

Send my roots rain

A poet once said 'send my roots rain' and this is how I feel now, Lord! I am dry and empty, and even the thought of you leaves me unmoved. The whole of nature seems to blossom and be fruitful, and only I am dry, parched, bored. Give me courage to keep on and give me the hope that you will water my dry soul so that life for me again will be joyous and fruitful.

Reading: Ezek 37:1-14 The dry bones.

You are wonderful

Lord, you are wonderful beyond all words, all thoughts, emotions, all imaginings!

You are more wonderful than anything that I have ever known. You are stillness, you are wayless, you are light, you are joy, you are the fullness of all things — yet you are more wonderful than all these! If only there were words to express what you are, if there were images to describe you or music to suggest the magic of your being! All descriptions are only smudged shadows of your reality.

You are wonderful beyond all things and yet you have touched me with yourself so that I have glimpsed the wonder, the greatness, the

133

mysteriousness of you which are beyond description!
Reading: Ps 84 How my soul yearns and pines.

AUGUST 20

The feast of St. Bernard

Love is the result of love, it is intrinsically valuable. I love because I love; I love in order to love. Love is a valuable thing only if it returns to its beginning, consults its origin and flows back to its source . . . When God loves, he wishes only to be loved in return, assuredly he loves for no other purpose than to be loved. He knows that those who love are happy in their love.

St. Bernard (1090-1153)
from *On the Song of Songs*

Reading: Song 1:1-4 How right it is to love you.

AUGUST 21

Be still

'Be still then, and know that I am God'; it isn't easy for us to be still! Teach me, Lord, to quieten my busy mind, to dissolve the pictures my imagination builds up, the memories which keep re-occuring so that the knowledge of your being is all that I am concerned with. You are all that matters in the world and in my life; help me to be still with the sense of your presence and of your penetrating love.   Amen.

Reading: Ps 63 You satisfy my soul.

AUGUST 22

Touch me with your glory

Lord you are glorious,
You are wonderful,
Beyond all I can imagine
I want to praise,
To thank you
But words fail me.
Touch me with your

Glory so that it
Changes my drabness,
My meanness into
The likeness of your Son
Whose whole being
Was lit by the fire of love.
Light up my life
With love that burns
For you, your world,
And all your creatures.

Reading: Rev 15:1-14 How great and wonderful are all your works.

Stillness in a busy world

We try to flee from you, Lord, but you are in the end inescapable. I want to stop running and yield myself to you but so many things get in the way. There seems to be no time to be alone with you; there is no silence in the world around me or in my life. Even on holiday by the sea or on the hills, people take radios or tape-recorders with them, and in a car nose to tail with others, there is no peace. So many people are trying to get away from themselves and from you.

Today we try to keep busy, and keep rushing ahead. In a restless world, Lord, it is difficult not to get caught in the flight away from you. Catch me in your stillness and peace; surround me with them, put them in my heart so that even in the bustle of today's world I know that I am yours and that I cannot escape from you!

Reading: 1 Sam 3:1-15 Samuel learns to listen to God.

The feast of St. Bartholomew, apostle

We remember today your apostle Bartholomew and all other followers of yours about whom little is known, though the Church honours them. So many people live close to you in love and by their unassuming goodness show forth your glory in the world; but the secular world takes little notice of them because they have no news value. Increase our faith and love of you so that like Saint Bartholomew we follow the way your Son Jesus Christ leads, and by doing so, show forth your glory by serving those who live round about us.   Amen.

Reading: Lk 22:24-30 Service of others.

Life as praise of God

Fill Thou my life, O Lord my God,
In every part with praise,
That my whole being may proclaim
Thy being and Thy ways.

Praise in the common things of life;
Its goings out and in:
Praise in each duty and each deed
however small and mean.

Fill every part of me with praise;
Let all my being speak
Of Thee and of thy love, O Lord,
Poor though I be and weak.

So shall each fear, each fret, each care
Be turned into song;
And every winding of the way
The echo shall prolong.

So shall no part of day or night
From sacredness be free;
But all my life, in every step,
Be fellowship with Thee.

Horatio Bonar (1808-1889)

Reading: Col 1:3-14 The kind of life the Lord expects of you.

AUGUST 26

With thee we are rich

Thou art the source and centre of all minds,
Their only point of rest, eternal Word!
From thee departing, they are lost and rove
At random, without honour, hope, or peace.
From Thee is all that soothes the life of man,
His high endeavour, and his glad success,
His strength to suffer, and his will to serve.
But oh! Thou bounteous Giver of all good,
Thou art of all Thy gifts Thyself the Crown!
Give what Thou canst, without Thee we are poor,
And with Thee rich, take what thou wilt away.

William Cowper (1731-1800)

Reading: Dan 3:51-90 Song of the three young men, or Ps 107:1-22 Thank the Lord for his
steadfast love.

The feast of St. Monica, Mother of St. Augustine
Saint Augustine and his mother Monica, standing by a window overlooking a garden at Ostia, talked about you, Lord, and eternal life as the saints know it. You seem momentarily to have lifted them up into it. Augustine, usually a master of words, struggles to describe the experience. He tells us that they soared high by inward musing, by talking about you and your creation, by regarding their own souls. Then you took them further to the region of never failing plenty. Trying to describe the experience and how it may happen, he and his mother said: 'If to any man the tumults of the flesh be silenced, if the fancies of the earth be silenced; if the poles of heaven be silenced also; if the very soul be silent to herself, and by forgetting self, surmount self . . . then we may hear him we love without any means of creatures, and in swift thought touch on that eternal Wisdom which is over all. If this exultation of spirit could last for ever, it would truly be entering into our Master's joy.'

Reading: 2 Cor 12:1-10 St. Paul's experience of the third heaven.

The feast of St. Augustine
Late have I loved thee, O thou eternal truth and goodness, late have I sought thee, my Father! But thou didst seek me, and when thou shinest forth upon me, then I knew thee and learnt to love thee. I thank thee, O my light, that thou didst thus shine upon me; that thou didst teach my soul what thou wouldst be to me, and didst incline thy face in pity unto me, thou, Lord, hast become my hope, my comfort, my strength, my all! In thee doth my soul rejoice. The darkness vanished before mine eyes, and I beheld thee, the sun of righteousness. When I loved darkness, I knew thee not, but wandered on from night to night. But thou didst lead me out of that blindness; thou didst take me by the hand and call me to thee, and now I can thank thee, and thy mighty voice which hath penetrated to my inmost heart.

St. Augustine (354-430)
from *The Confessions*

Reading: Hos 5:15 and 6:1-6 Come let us return to the Lord.

The commemoration of the beheading of St. John the Baptist
John gave himself so completely to the service of your word, Lord, he did not fear to stand firm against the evil in Herod. For this he paid with his

life. Your love asks each of us to respond with our love by giving ourselves freely and fully. Put into my heart today, Lord, a knowledge of your will for me and the strength to live that life in joy.

Reading: Lk 6:39-45 Out of the fullness of the heart.

AUGUST 30

For strangers and exiles

No one is a stranger to you, Lord. We are never out of your sight. In your kindness watch over refugees and exiles, those separated from their loved ones, young people who are lost or who have run away from home. Lead them safely through the dangers of city and countryside. And Lord, keep us open to recognise and love them with a share of your kindness, so that they will be lost and exiled and strangers no more.

Reading: Lk 6:36-38 Compassion and generosity.

AUGUST 31

Remembering the Celtic missionaries

I am grateful for the Celtic missionaries from Ireland and today I thank you particularly for Saint Aidan who left the peace of Iona to come to preach and teach the Christian faith in Northern England. He was generous to the poor and freed slaves in an age when this was rare. There is so much in his life that I praise you for and I ask you to help me, like him to show forth the light of the gospel of your son by being gentle, moderate and good. People in our pagan world today are not so much touched by words as by the way we live. Give me the grace to live as a true follower of your Son who gave us his life in obedience to your will for us and our salvation.

Reading: Mt 28:18-20 The commission to preach.

September

Back to work, back to school,
with thanks for the goodness of God in the harvest

In Europe, where we are compiling this book, the holiday season of the summer months begins to come to an end in September. Schools come back into session, work begins to pick up again, the harvest is in mid-course, the evenings are drawing in.

After the relaxation of August we can begin to gear ourselves into Autumn and Winter. In many ways, these are the months when we can get down to a little more bookwork, to a study or discussion group, even to a more settled routine for prayer, perhaps.

It is as well, at the same time, that we should not just be parochial. We may be able to remember that this can be a period when some areas, such as India, can be subjected to intense threat from hurricane and flood. As we rejoice in the harvest, others may be hit by famine or annihilation. We could pause a moment to reflect that if we are concerned with a new school year, or getting in the crops, or taking up work again after a break, there are those who, practically speaking, have no school, those who slave at parched soil to scrape together enough to starve on, those who have been unemployed all their adult life and face another year of human degradation.

Through all this . . . somehow . . . comes the glory of God. And we must live out our lives where we are, in the situation which prevails, while trying to expand our minds and hearts to those who are less fortunate than we are.

So, we can pray this month in gratitude for the gifts of God, for his glory and his goodness. We can ask for all the help and strength we need to get on with a new school year, whether as teacher, parent, or child. In the midst of this, as though to remind us of our daily living, we celebrate the feast of the Triumph of the Cross, with all that this triumph means in the interpretation of want, diseases, calamity, persecution and all the great and small emergencies of our human lives.

For us, this month can underline the complexity of God's creation, the growing together of the good and bad until the harvest. The coming of Michaelmas at the end of the month stresses the constant warfare between good and evil which reigns in our own minds, hearts and bodies, in the yearly development of nature, in the relationship of men and women in the world, in the councils of the nations.

Indeed, as we rejoice at God's abundance, at the hope there is in the educational programme for more and more people, we can realise more deeply how much God relies upon us to cooperate with him . . . literally to make his creation bear fruit.

The Lord is everywhere

Where I wander — You!
Where I ponder — You!
Only You, You again, always You!
You! You! You!
When I am gladdened — You!
When I am saddened — You!
Only You, You again, always You!
You! You! You!
Sky is You, earth is You!
You above! You below!
In every trend, at every end,
Only you, you again, always You!
You! You! You!

Levi Yitzchak of Berditchev (*c.* 1740-1810)
from *Forms of Prayer for Jewish Worship*

Reading: Ps 139:7-12 We cannot escape from you.

God's glory

'The heavens show forth the glory of God.' Living in the country, Lord, I find it easy to look at the sky, the sun, the moon and the stars. They open me up to a sense of the infinite you. Thank you for that. But in the city where I live, there is so much noise and dirt, smoke and stench, rudeness and rush, I find it hard to look at the glory of the sky I can hardly catch a glimpse of. Yet we men and women have made this mixture of beauty and mess in your world. It is hard to believe we are the glory of your creation. As we walk about and look round we ask you to teach us about yourself and what your glory really is.

Reading: Ps 19

The feast of St. Gregory the Great

O God, who for our redemption didst give thine only begotten Son to the death of the cross, and by his glorious resurrection has delivered us from the power of the enemy, grant us to die daily to sin, that we may evermore live with him, in the joy of his resurrection; through the same Jesus Christ our Lord.

St. Gregory (c. 540-604)

Reading: Col 2:8-15 Christ died that we might be a new creation, made alive again.

SEPTEMBER 4

Modern idea of the Lord is my shepherd

The Lord is my Pace-setter, I shall not rush.
He makes me stop and rest for quiet intervals.
He provides me with images of stillness which restore my serenity.
He leads me in ways of efficiency through calmness of mind and his
    guidance is peace.
Even though I have a great many things to accomplish each day I will not
    fret,
For His presence is here, His timelessness, His all importance will keep
    me in balance.
He prepares refreshment and renewal, in the midst of my activity.
By anointing my mind with His oils of tranquility my cup of joyous
    energy overflows.
Surely harmony and effectiveness shall be the fruits of my hours,
For I shall walk in the pace of my Lord, and dwell in His house for ever.
Glory be to the Father, and to the Son,
And to the Holy Spirit.
As it was in the beginning, is now, and ever shall be, world without end.
    Amen.

Toki Miyashina

Reading: Ps 23 The Lord is my Shepherd.

SEPTEMBER 5

God is with us always

Lord, be with our spirit, and dwell in our hearts by faith. Oh! make us such as we should be towards thee, and such as thou mayest take pleasure in us. Be with us everywhere and at all times, in all events and circumstances of our life, to sanctify and sweeten to us whatever befalls us; and never leave or forsake us in our present pilgrimage here, till thou has brought us safe through all trials and dangers to be ever with thee, there to live in thy sight and love, world without end.   Amen.

Benjamin Jenks (1646-1724)

Reading: Eph 3:13-19 Dwell in our hearts by faith.

Take me where you will
Come, Lord, come with me; see with my eyes, hear with my ears; think with my mind; love with my heart — in all situations of my life.

Work with my hands, my strength. Take, cleanse, possess, inhabit my will, my understanding, my love. Take me where you will, to do what you want, in your way.

Evelyn Underhill (1875-1941)
from *Meditations and Prayers*

Reading: Prov 6:6-22 When you walk, these will guide you.

Your words calm me down.
'Peace be still' is the most wonderful thing you ever said, Lord! It calms me down when I want to lash out at those who hurt me with words; it stops my jitters when I'm afraid of people; it slows down my mind when it is panicking about all the things I have to do with so little time for them. Most important, it makes me quiet so that I can hear your still small voice when it speaks to me so gently.

Thank you.

Reading: Mk 4:36-41 Jesus calms the storm.

Birthday of Mary
In thinking of the birth of Mary, we can think also of your birth, Jesus Christ. Mary loved God and gave herself to be filled with your love. Hers was then a mother's love, real, human, tangible, filled with joy and pain. May we learn from you and from her the varied colours of human love.

Amen.

Reading: Lk 2:41-52 Jesus and his parents.

The value of the daily round
Up again this morning, Lord. The same old round. It is a hard thing to feel the future stretching out ahead with an endless succession of getting up, working, going to bed and getting up again. How can you teach me the value of this daily round. Why is it that I am always wanting change, wanting something new? Your world goes on for centuries and centuries with such small, slow changes. But my life is short and small. There does not seem to be time to go so slowly. I want movement. I want growth. I want to see what I am making of life. I want a sense of achievement. Am I

143

wrong in all this, Lord, because you did make me with a head and a desire to develop? Isn't growth something you want from us too? Give me the understanding to balance speed and slowness, progress and stillness. In You, they are somehow one.

Reading: Job 38:1-40:5 Who is obscuring my designs with his empty headed words?

SEPTEMBER 10

When school begins again

The daily round is beginning again, holidays are over and winter lies ahead; teachers get busy again and parents have more time on their hands; grandparents miss their grandchildren's visits. The pattern of life gets back to normal and it can seem dull and monotonous. Show us, Lord, that there is a challenge in every situation and that you are with us supporting us whatever happens, ready to change the ordinary into the miraculous.

Reading: Eccles 3:1-8 There is a time for everthing.

SEPTEMBER 11

A prayer for teachers and pupils

The new school year is starting up. We pray for those who teach and those who learn, and for the parents of school children. Help them to grow in understanding of each other, and to give of their best, and to realize the joys of discovering new facts, of how things work, and the pleasure of making new friends. Take away and break down barriers so that both the teachers and the taught may learn more about each other and themselves, and may come to know more about you and your will for the world today.   Amen.

Reading: Prov 2:1-15 The Lord gives wisdom.

SEPTEMBER 12

Advice for teachers

There is no credit in spending all your affection on the cream of your pupils. Try rather to bring more troublesome ones to order, by using gentleness. Nobody can heal every wound with the same unguent, where there are acute spasms of pain, we have to apply soothing poultices. So in all circumstances be wise as the serpent, though always as harmless as the dove.

St. Ignatius of Antoich (+*c.* 107)
from his *Letter to Polycarp*

Reading: Eph 4:1-7 There is one body and one Spirit.

The feast of St. Cyprian

God is present everywhere, he hears and sees all, he penetrates even hidden and secret places. For so it is written 'I am a God at hand, and not a God afar off. If a man hides himself in secret places, will I therefore not see him? Do I not fill heaven and earth?'And again: 'The eyes of the Lord are in every place, keeping watch on the evil and the good.'

St. Cyprian (*c.* 200-258)
from *On the Lord's Prayer*

Reading: Mt 6:7-10 Our Father

The Cross

Though Christ a thousand times
In Bethlehem be born,
If he's not born in thee
Thy soul is still forlorn.
The cross on Golgotha
Will never save thy soul,
The cross in thine own heart
Alone can make thee whole.

Angelus Silesius (1624-1677)

Reading: Mt 16:24-28 Christ's followers must take up their cross.

How can I bless those who persecute me?

The scripture says: 'Bless those who persecute you: bless and do not curse them.' What a thing to ask! How can I get to that stage of perfection? I seem always to be full of criticism for everyone except myself. But each day people niggle me. They criticise and condemn. Sometimes I feel nothing I do can ever be right. Is this what you mean? Bless them for showing me that I am bound to fail? Bless them for showing me I cannot win? Bless them for showing me I am powerless? Well, all right Lord, provided you can teach me also how strong you are, how you support and encourage, how you love. Do that Lord, and I will make a shot at blessing those who persecute.

Reading: Mt 18:1-10 Unless you change and become like little children you will never enter into the Kingdom of heaven.

Thanksgiving for God's gifts and
a prayer for the hungry of the world

We thank you, Lord and Creator of all things, for the blessings of this life and the great variety of your gifts, for the food we eat and the pleasure it gives us.

But we know that millions have less than enough while others eat to excess.

Food is wasted while millions starve.

Nature's resources are misused to bring men profit.

Forgive us, Lord, our selfishness, and open our hearts to the needs of the hungry wherever they may be, for the sake of our Lord Jesus Christ.

Basil Naylor
from *Contemporary Parish Prayers* (1975)

Reading: Mt 25:31-46 The parable of the sheep and the goats.

Harvest thanksgiving

Almighty God, creator of all things, at this time we praise and thank you for the harvest of grain and root crops, and of fruit and garden vegetables which are being gathered in. Without your providential care all our work and skills would be useless and we are truly grateful to you.

Help us never to forget that we are fellow workers with you in all we do as well as being stewards of your creation; give us a sense of responsibility for creation and for our fellow human beings. We ask this through Jesus Christ, who offers us the living bread which will never perish.

Amen.

Reading: Gen 1:26-31 God creates man, all living creatures and plants.

A prayer of thanks

God, our Father, we thank you for the world, and for all your gifts to us, for the sky above, the earth beneath our feet, and the wonderful process which provides food to maintain life. We thank you for our crops, and for the skills and techniques needed to grow and use them properly. Help us to use your gifts in the spirit of the giver, through Jesus Christ our Lord.

Amen.

J. R. Wordsall
from *Contemporary Parish Prayers* (1975)

Reading: Ps 104:1-23 Thanksgiving for God and his gifts.

For those less blessed than ourselves

At our harvest festivals our churches look beautiful, decorated with bunches of flowers, and piles of fruit and vegetables which have been grown in our gardens; we have every reason to praise you and thank you for your goodness. Help us also now and always to remember and try to help all the people who have no gardens or allotments where they can grow things or parks or playgrounds for their children; and also we remember the old who have no one to assist them with the care of their gardens. Show us how we can better help one another.   Amen.

Reading: Joel 2:21-27 God will provide for those who lack now.

The fruits of the Spirit

Dear Lord, when I look at the list of the fruits of the Spirit which Saint Paul talks about, I am greatly discouraged; love, joy, peace, patience and they go on ! I do not seem to start to have these qualities. Then I see that they are fruits of the Spirit; they are something which will grow in me if I open my whole being to the Holy Spirit. It is you, Lord, who will make them grow in me; you will do the work if I provide the soil. Here I am, sow the seeds of love, joy, peace, patience, kindness in me so that I may bear fruit for you and for the use of your people on earth.   Amen.

Reading: Gal 5:16-23 The fruits of the Spirit.

The feast of St. Matthew, evangelist

You choose very different kinds of people as your followers, Lord. Today we think of your apostle Matthew, a despised tax collector. You did not despise him but gave him your love and the honour of writing the Good News you preached. From this lesson, may we refuse to despise or look down on anyone, teach us humility. And, Lord, help those who work in tax offices and with money as the centre of their daily round.

Reading: Mt 9:9-13 Call of Matthew.

A thought on taxes and tax collectors

In the Gospel story, the tax collectors come in for some contempt, but you ate with them, Lord Jesus. I find it easy to get angry with tax people, There is always a desire to cheat them. Taxes often seem unfair and ridiculously high. I ask you today, Lord, that governments locally nationally and internationally may try to cut unnecessary expense, help the poor and work together for justice to the downtrodden.

Reading: Rom 13:1-7 On taxes.

SEPTEMBER 23

The loveliness of the world

We thank you, Lord, for the beauty and diversity of the world which you have made to be the home and mother of mankind.

We thank you for making its hospitality to man endless in interest, loveliness, diversity and utility.

Teach us by your creation to know more of you our Creator, and rejoicing in you, be as generous to others as you are to us; through Jesus Christ our Lord.

Dick Williams

Reading: Is 40:9-3 God the Creator and Ruler of the earth cares for us.

SEPTEMBER 24

Take me over

Lord Jesus, unite me to yourself in sacrifice.
Take my life in your hands
and offer it to God and mankind.
Empty me into your chalice as wine poured out.
Break me like bread in your hands
and share me as you will.
Do with me whatever you please.
Drown me in your blood and wash my sins.
Let me die to myself
and be reborn to you and to your brothers.
Give me to God and to others
as you give yourself;
for I am a member of your body.

Monk of the Eastern Church
from *The Unity Book of Prayers* (1969)

Reading: Cor 5:16-21 God through Christ reconciled us to himself and gave us the Ministry of reconcilation.

SEPTEMBER 25

Today

Look to this day, for it is life,
the very life of life.

148

In its brief course lie all the realities and truth of existence —
the joy of growth, the splendour of action, the glory of power.
For yesterday is but a memory, and tomorrow is only a vision,
But today well lived
Makes every yesterday a memory of happiness
and every tomorrow a vision of hope.
Look well, therefore, to this day.   Sanskrit Poem

Reading: Lk 12:13-21 A man's life is not made secure
                     by what he owns.

That I may see the needs of other people

The balance of what is rich and what is poor is very hard to understand.
But it is more than possible to know when men, women and children are
dying of undernourishment. Here it is also possible to be blind, by
looking more at my own personal needs, according to my standard,
which may unthinkingly include unnecessary luxuries, while others are
totally without basic necessities. Well then, Lord God of the harvest, help
me to look up and understand the desperate needs beyond myself and my
world.

Reading: Lk 12:16-21 On hoarding possessions.

Christ's relationship with the poor

Christ chose to be born in poverty and took poor men as his disciples; he
himself became the servant of the poor and so shared their condition that
whatever good or harm was done to the poor, he said he would consider
done to himself. Since God loves the poor, he also loved the lovers of the
poor; when someone loves another, he loves too those who love or serve
the other.

St. Vincent de Paul (1580-1660)

Reading: Mt 25:37-40 You did to the least.

War against evil

Almighty God, sovereign of all creation, we praise your name for men
and angels who have joined in the war against the powers of evil.

Most of all we praise you for the cross of your Son Jesus Christ
which ensures the final victory.

149

Grant that we who are marked with the sign of the victory may continue Christ's faithful soldiers and servants to our lives' end.

Basil Naylor
from *Contemporary Parish Prayers* (1975)

Reading: Rom 8:38-39 The victory of Christ over all principalities and powers.

SEPTEMBER 29

The feast of St. Michael, archangel

Whenever a mighty deed is in question, Michael is assigned, so that by his actions and name (Who-is-like-God) it may be made known that no one can do what God can do. So in the case of our ancient enemy who in his pride wanted to be like God . . . when he is shown to be condemned to eternal punishment at the end of the world, he is described as about to do battle with Michael, as Saint John says: War broke out with Michael the Archangel.

St. Gregory the Great (*c.* 540-604)
from *On the Gospels*

Reading: Rev 12:11-12 Michael battles with Satan.

SEPTEMBER 30

The feast of St. Jerome

If, as the apostle Paul says, Christ is the power of God and the wisdom of God, then he who is ignorant of the scriptures is also ignorant of the power of God and his wisdom; ignorance of the scriptures is ignorance of Christ.

St. Jerome (*c.* 342-420)
from *On the Prophet Isaiah*

Reading: 2 Tim 3:14-17 The Holy scriptures . . . from these you can learn wisdom.

October

The Lord's harvest in the saints
approached through deep prayer
and illustrated through the life of St. Luke

'Season of mists and mellow fruitfulness'. The English poet expresses the feel of Autumn in his own country in this beautiful line. Though it is not Autumn in large areas of the world when we come to October, there is a certain sense of harvest which pervades the liturgy of the month, wherever anyone may be. It is a season of saints, a season of greatly different people finding their way to the Pauline statement: 'You will with all the saints have strength to grasp the breadth and length, the height and depth, until knowing the love of Christ, which is beyond all knowledge, you are filled with the utter fullness of God.' (Eph 3:18-18 [JB]).

Because of this, we decided that it would be good to dwell in prayer on the very richness of those who are and have been our brothers and sisters in the human race. Looking at them, listening to them, coming to understand a little more what they were about, we can hope confidently to make progress ourselves in the way of the saints, the spiritual life.

The month begins remembering a young girl of the last century who died when she was only twenty-four after living almost all her life in a small French town, and much of that life in an enclosed Carmelite convent. Theresa of Lisieux was a saint of simplicity, and she is followed in the calendar by that early medieval saint of great appeal, Francis of Assisi. Almost immediately after that comes the feast of Saint Bruno, who founded the toughest and most enclosed of all religious orders, the Carthusians. This silent and tiny group of men lived apart to give themselves totally to God in solitary prayer and contemplation, a very different life from that of Saint Denis who was bishop of Paris and a martyr. Perhaps the whole of this variety of saints is summed up by two

151

feasts later in the month. First there is Saint Luke who wrote so graphically and so profoundly of the Christ he had never known personally, and yet whom he knew intimately enough from the dynamic Church at Antioch. Saint Luke is the author of what might be called 'the gospel of prayer'. Secondly, there is the feast of Saint Simon and Saint Jude, almost the 'unknown apostles', stressing for us that sanctity does not have to be visible or known to us but is the reality of our relationship of love with God, Father, Son and Holy Spirit.

Fittingly this month moves towards the celebration at the beginning of November of All Saints. In studying and praying with the wonderfully varied saints of October we become more and more aware that we, too, are called to be saints.

The feast of St. Theresa of Lisieux

I was still being tormented by this question of unfulfilled longings for martyrdom and it was a distraction in my prayer, when I decided to consult Saint Paul's epistles in the hope of getting an answer. It was the twelfth and thirteenth chapters of the First Corinthians that claimed my attention ... When Saint Paul was talking about the different members of the mystical body I couldn't recognise myself in any of them; or rather I could recognise myself in all of them. But charity — that was the key to my vocation. If the Church was a body composed of different members, it couldn't lack the noblest of all; it must have a heart, and a heart burning with love. I realised that this love was the true motive force which enabled the other members of the Church to act; if it ceased to function the apostles would forget to preach the gospel; the martyrs would refuse to shed their blood. Love, in fact, is the vocation which includes all others ... Beside myself with joy, I cried out: 'Jesus, my love! I've found my vocation, and my vocation is love.'

St. Theresa of Lisieux (1873-1897)
from *Autobiography*

Reading: 1 Cor 12:12-31 The analogy of the body.

Guardian Angels

'He has given his angels charge over you, to guard you in all your ways.' Let the Lord be thanked for his steadfast love, his wonderful works to the sons of men. Let the nations praise him and say the Lord has done great things for them ... And that no being in heaven may rest from the work of caring for us, you send those blessed spirits to minister to us, assign them to watch over us, you bid them to be our guardians.

St. Bernard (1090-1153)
from a *Sermon*

Reading: Tob 12:6-22 I am Raphael, or Rev 19:9-10 Our fellow servants.

The Blessing of Brother Leo

May God bless you and keep you.
May God smile on you, and be merciful to you;

may God turn his regard towards you and give you peace.
May God bless you, Brother Leo.

St. Francis of Assisi (*c.* 1181-1226)

Reading: Jn 14:27-24 Christ's peace.

OCTOBER 4

The feast of St. Francis of Assisi

Lord make me an instrument of thy peace,
Where there is hatred, let me sow love;
Where there is injury, pardon;
Where there is doubt, faith;
Where there is despair, hope,
Where there is darkness, light; and
Where there is sadness, joy.
O Divine Master, grant that I may not so much seek to be consoled as to
    console;
To be understood as to understand,
To be loved as to love,
For it is in giving that we receive;
It is in pardoning that we are pardoned.
And it is in dying that we are born to eternal life.

St. Francis of Assisi (*c.* 1181-1226)

Reading: 2 Cor 1:3-7 Christ's comfort.

OCTOBER 5

The Canticle of Brother Sun

Most high, all-powerful, all good, Lord
All praise is yours, all glory, all honour and all blessing.
All praise be yours, my Lord, through all that you have made,
And first my Lord Brother Sun,
Who brings the day; and light you give to us through him.
How beautiful is he, how radiant in all his splendour!
To you, Most High, he bears the likeness.
All praise be yours, my Lord, through sister Moon and Stars;
In the heavens you have made them, bright
And precious and fair.
All praise by yours, my Lord, through Brothers Wind and Air,
And fair and stormy, all the weather's moods,
By which you cherish all that you have made.
All praise be yours, my Lord, through Sister Water,
So useful, lowly, precious and pure.

All praise be yours, My Lord, through Brother Fire,
Through whom you give light in darkness.
How beautiful is he, how gay! Full of strength and power.
All praise be yours, my Lord, through Sister Earth, our mother,
Who feeds in her sovereignty and produces
Various fruits with coloured flower and herbs.
All praise be yours, my Lord, for those who grant pardon
For love of you; for those who endure
Sickness and trial.
Happy are those who endure in peace,
By you, Most High, they will be crowned.
All praise be yours, my Lord, through Sister Death,

From whose embarce no mortal can escape.
Woe to those who die in mortal sin!
Happy those She finds doing your will!
The second death can do no harm to them!
Praise and bless my Lord, and give him thanks,
And serve him with great humility.

St. Francis of Assisi (c. 1181-1226)

Reading: Ps 19 The heavens tell of the glory of God.

OCTOBER 6

The feast of St. Bruno, founder of the Carthusian Order

We are grateful to men like Saint Bruno who have sought you in the quietness and solitude of the countryside, and who have imparted to others something of the wonder of knowing you in depth. Encourage us to build an interior cell, a holy ground and a holy place wherein you and your servant speak often together, as a man speaketh to his friend; wherein often the faithful soul is joined to your Word, and heavenly things mix with earthly.[1] Lord, show me how to build such a cell in my heart 'a cell of self knowledge and of knowledge of you'[2] where even at the busiest times of my life I may commune with you undisturbed and may know as a reality that 'Brother body is our cell and the soul sits there like a hermit and thinks on God and prays to Him.'[3]   Amen.

1. The Golden Epistle of William of St. Thierry
written to a community of Carthusians
2. St. Catherine of Siena
3. St. Francis of Assisi

Reading: Jer 31:31-34 God promises us hearts to know him.

OCTOBER 7

They have the love of God before them

They (Good men) have the love of God before them in their inward seeing, as a common good pouring forth through heaven and earth; and they feel the Holy Trinity inclined towards them, within them, with fullness of grace. And therefore they are adorned without and within with all the virtues, with holy practices and with good works. Thus they are united with God through Divine grace and their own holy lives. And because they have abandoned themselves to God in doing, in leaving undone, and in suffering, they have steadfast peace and inward joy, consolation and savour of which the world cannot partake . . . Moreover those same inward men have before them in their inward seeing whenever they will, the love of God as something drawing them or urging them into the Unity . . .

> John of Ruysbroeck (1293-1381)
> from *The Book of Supreme Truth*

Reading: Song 8:6-7 Love.

OCTOBER 8

He is nearer to us than we think

Lift up your heart to him, sometimes even at your meals and when you are in company; the least little remembrance will always be acceptable to him. You need not cry very loud; he is nearer to us than we are aware of. We may make an oratory of our heart wherein to retire from time to time, to converse with hm in meekness, humility and love.

> Brother Lawrence (1624-1691)

Reading: Ps 139:1-8 You examine me and you know me.

OCTOBER 9

The remembrance of St. Denis and Dionysius

We thank you for Saint Denis of Paris, missionary and martyr at Montmartre, and for that mysterious writer called Dionysius (or Denis) the Areopagite, both of whom we remember today. Inspire us to come to know you in that close way that these men did by surrendering the whole of ourselves, bodies, minds and souls to you so that by losing our lives we may find true life in you. Lord, it is not easy to put a cloud of forgetting between ourselves and the busy world when we come to pray and to offer ourselves to you; show us how, with firm, devout intent, to turn to you and come to know you in love, for we realise that by love you may be reached when thinking fails. IIelp us to understand that it is only the

156

splendour of light that hides you from our vision and this is why we only know you now in a kind of 'dazzling darkness'.

Reading: Ex 24:12-18 Moses' encounter with God in the cloud.

Can you hear me, Lord?

Day passes, night comes; morning comes, day passes, night comes... this is our life and our living, Lord. You are the maker of day and night. You rule the sun, the moon and the stars. I often do not find it easy or of any meaning to tell myself that you are about when day passes and night comes and everything goes on rather like clockwork. It is so impersonal, Lord. I feel I want to shout out: 'Can you hear me, Lord?' . . . and sometimes I do. And still you are silent, and morning comes, day passes — where are you Lord?

And the Lord answers: 'I am in your heart'.

Reading: Eccles 3:1-8 There is a season for everything, a time for every occupation under heaven.

An understanding heart

Grant me, O Lord, an understanding hear, that I may see into the hearts of thy people, and know their strengths and weaknesses, their hopes and their despairs, their efforts and failures, their need of love and their need to love. Through my touch with them grant them comfort and hope, and the assurance that new life begins at any age and on any day, redeeming the past, sanctifying the present, and brightening the future with the assurance of thy unfailing love, brought to me in Jesus Christ, thy Son my Lord.

George Appleton
from *One Man's Prayers*

Reading: 1 Kings 3:5-14 God gives Solomon an understanding heart.

Friendship with the saints

Lord, it is hard to explain to people how I know in a real way some of your saints who are living in glory with you. Some seem to be particularly near to me and, like my friends on earth, support me in difficult situations. Perhaps we share a similar love for you or perhaps we had similar backgrounds, or perhaps like human friends, we just hit it off. I thank you for these friendships with the saints and ask you to widen our knowledge and love of your followers whether they are in this world or the next.

Reading: 1 Jn 1:1-10 Our fellowship with Christ and one another.

OCTOBER 13

The feast of St. Edward, King and Confessor.

When we venerate Saint Edward, we venerate a failure. We do so advisedly. Not because success in life necessarily falls to the grasping and unscrupulous, so that success itself should be mistrusted by Christians as a sign of rascality ... But because we will not let ourselves be blinded by the lure of worldly success so as to forget that the true statesmanship is exercised in the council chamber, and the true warfare fought on the battlefield of the human soul.

Ronald Knox (1888-1957)
from a *Sermon*

Reading: Heb 12:1-4 So many witnesses in a great cloud.

OCTOBER 14

Forgive and heal us

O Spirit of God,
Set at rest the crowded, hurrying, conscious thoughts within our minds
and hearts.
Let the peace and quiet of your presence take possession of us.
Help us to relax, to rest, to become open and receptive to you.
You know our inmost spirits the hidden unconscious life within us
the forgotten memories of hurts and fears the frustrated desires
the unresolved tensions and dilemmas.
Cleanse and sweeten the springs of our being
that freedom, life and love may flow into both our conscious and hidden
life.
Lord, we lie open before you, waiting for your healing, your peace and
your word.

George Appleton
from *Jerusalem Prayers for the World Today*

Reading: Mk 2:1-14 The healing of the paralytic.

OCTOBER 15

The feast of St. Teresa of Avila

Let nothing disturb you,
Let nothing afright you,
All things pass;
God never changes
Patience gains all things.
He who has God
Can wait for nothing.
God alone suffices.

St. Teresa of Avila (1515-1582)

Reading: Rom 8:31-39 With God on our side ...

Where God is to be found

The soul which is once well entered, and elevated by the means of abnegation for the will of God, both in and out of prayer, shall find no great difficulty afterwards, but shall at all times enter in again as having undone the knot, found the secret and dived to the depth of the whole matter; as having by experience found God the true light, joy and life, not where she thought, nor where men ordinarily seek him, namely in ourselves or in our own proper will, nor in seeking our own delight, joy, light and comfort; but where commonly men never seek him, namely in renouncing ourselves, yea and our spiritual joy, consolation, and light, putting them as it were, out of mind for the actual remembrance and great joy which the soul hath of the will of God and to do his pleasure.

Benet of Canfield (1584-1610)
from The Rule of Perfection

Reading: Mk 8:34-37 The renouncing of self.

The feast of St. Ignatius of Antioch

Given a thorough going faith and love for Jesus Christ, there is nothing at all that will not be obvious to you; for life begins and ends with those two qualities. Faith is the beginning, and love is the end; and the union of the two together is God.

St. Ignatius of Antioch (+107)
from his Letter to the Ephesians

Reading: Col 3:11-17 There is only Christ.

The feast of St. Luke

O Lord, the healer of all our diseases, who knows that the sick have need of a physician; bless all whom you have called to be sharers in your own work of healing with health alike of body and soul, that they may learn their art in dependence upon you, and exercise it always under thy sanction, and to your honour and glory, who live and reign with the Holy Spirit, ever one God, world without end.

Sursum Corda (19th century)

Reading: Is 55 Listen, and your soul will live.

The Church's healing mission

Luke as a physician tried to heal the body but through his writings

159

provided a medicine for the soul. We, your church, so often leave your healing mission in the hands of doctors and nurses and forget the soul requires your healing touch even more than the body. We all need you, Lord Jesus, to unite our fragmented natures which are pulled in so many directions and in which good and evil war with each other. Give us interior harmony and bring to our soul your peace so that we will be better able to extend your healing mission to others as you asked us to do.

Amen.

Reading: Mk 16:14-20 Jesus tells us to go and preach and heal.

OCTOBER 20

The name of Jesus

Lord Jesus Christ have mercy on me a sinner! It is in your name, Lord Jesus Christ, that we are to heal; help us to have your name on our lips, in our minds and in our hearts so that we come to know you more deeply, and so that you may take over our lives and work through us. Come, Lord, come into our hearts and reign there!

Reading: Acts 4:5-12 The power of the name.

OCTOBER 21

The Church's task of communicating

Luke was expert at communicating the healing message of your Son Jesus Christ; you have given us, who are your church on earth, the task of continuing his work. Men and women in today's world are worn down by the pressures of life and its pace; and many feel that they are lonely and unloved, and they need the healing of your gospel. But Lord, it is hard to know how to get your message over or what words, or means to use. Show us how we start our dialogue with the needy and careworn; reveal to us more clearly the Word, who became flesh and dwelt among us.

Reading: Ex 4:10-16 God shows Moses how to use Aaron as his spokesman.

OCTOBER 22

You, Lord, cannot be captured

Lord, you communicate with us in many unexpected ways. Moses was surprised when you revealed yourself to him in a burning bush but this revelation was something he never forgot and deeply implanted in his heart and mind was your name, 'I am that I am' which you transmitted to him. He caught the meaning of the fire and the strange name — You, the Lord, cannot be captured in a form that stays the same; you will be in every situation as you will be! Help us to use pictures or verbal

160

illustrations when we try to tell people about you and your greatness and love for us in such a way that will not limit you to our restricted vision. Give to us, your people, wisdom and a sense of awe as you did to your servant Moses.

Reading: Ex 3:1-14 Moses and the burning bush.

How can we teach You, Lord?

Lord Jesus, you communicated to the people you talked with through stories which caught their interest; you held them spellbound. So often people find us boring when we try to tell them about you. Perhaps it was you, the Word, who fascinated them more than the stories; your sympathy and understanding touched them deeply. Work in us, give us new, loving, caring hearts, hearts like yours so that when we speak of you, the hearts of others will catch fire and the message will come alive.

Reading: Lk 10:25-37 One of Jesus' stories.

The Church — a reconciler

Grant, O God, that your church may increasingly become
    a reconciling force among peoples,
witnessing to the unity of all men
in the family of the one Father;
checking passion in time of strife,
reminding men of the ways of Christ,
and exhibiting above all things
that brotherhood of mankind taught by our Master,
Jesus Christ our Lord.

C. R. Forrester
from *Contemporary Parish Prayers*

Reading: Is 65:17-25 No more will the sound of weeping be heard.

The old being made new

O God of unchangeable power and eternal light, look favourably on the whole church, that wonderful and sacred mystery; and by the tranquil operation of thy perpetual providence, carry out the work of man's salvation; and let the whole world feel and see that things which were cast down are being raised up, and that those which had grown old are being made new, and that all things are returning to perfection, through him from whom they took their origin, even Jesus Christ thy Son our Lord.

From the Gelasian Sacramentary (late 7th century)

Reading: Rev 22:1-5 The healing of the nations.

OCTOBER 26

Christ guard me

Christ keep me safe, Christ guard me lowly,
Christ bring me to his dwelling high,
Christ give me strength, Christ make me holy,
Christ save me lest in hell I lie,
In life, in death God keep me whole
And bless my soul. This hope have I.

From the Irish

Reading: Rom 8:35-39 Who shall separate us from the love of Christ.

OCTOBER 27

That I may breathe freely

Lift up my soul above the weary round of harassing thoughts to thy eternal Presence. Lift up my soul to the pure, bright serene, radiant atmosphere of thy Presence, that there I may breathe freely, there repose in thy love, there be at rest from myself, and from all things that weary me; and thence return, arrayed with thy peace, to do and be what shall please thee.

E. B. Pusey (1800-1882)
from *Prayers*

Reading: 1 Thes 5:23-25 May the God of peace sanctify you.

OCTOBER 28

The feast of St. Simon and St. Jude

Jesus Christ, you chose Simon and Jude to be among your apostles and we are grateful for their witness to you though we know very little about their lives and how they served your church. We also remember today the many other humble, unspectacular people who have served you in a quiet, unobtrusive way by building up the body of the church among the small people of the world. Help us to learn from their example so that we, too, may extend your kingdom by our persistant following of the way you lead us, even if it seems to us to be humdrum and dull and unlikely to achieve very much.

Increase our faith and love, for you alone can keep us from falling, and you only can save us when danger and calamity threatens.

Amen.

Reading: Gal 6:1-5 Bearing one another's burdens.

162

If I hold thy hand in the darkness

As the rain hides the stars, as the autumn mist hides the hills as the clouds veil the blue of the sky, so the dark happenings of my lot hide the shining of thy face from me. Yet, if I may hold thy hand in the darkness, it is enough. Since I know that, though I may stumble in my going, thou dost not fall.

Alistair Maclean
from *Hebridean Altars*

Reading. Ps 121 Help comes to me from the Lord.

They shall see God

The blessedness of seeing God is rightly promised to those who are pure of heart. For the eye that is filled with dirt cannot see the brightness of true light; what is joy to the clear, shining mind is punishment to the mind which is stained. Let the darkness of the empty things of this world be set aside and the eyes of the soul be cleansed of all the filth of sin so that the inward sight may enjoy in peace the wonderful vision of God.

St. Leo the Great (+461)
from *On the Beatitudes*

Reading: Mt 5:8 Blessed are the pure of heart.

A thought and prayer for Hallowe'en

Here we are again remembering All Saints and All Souls. Lord, you know I am no saint! Yet the saints do encourage me. They were real men and women like ourselves, and they got the vision of Christ likeness. So help me, Lord, by your Spirit to become more and more like you. And the departed! What a lot of them there are! But some of them are my nears and dears. So strengthen me in what I really do believe — 'One family, we dwell in him, one Church above, beneath, though now divided by the narrow stream of death.' Thank you, O Lord Jesus, for being the Son of him who is the God of the living and departed.

Eric S. Abbott

Reading: Heb 12:1-4 A cloud of witnesses.

November

The Communion of Saints — here and in heaven
God's presence
The Lord of All Creation

November is the last month in the calendar of the Church's year. As such, it comes as a summing up of all creation which Saint Paul describes as groaning in its expectancy of the coming of the kingdom.

We begin the month with the feast of all the saints. In a way this is clear and simple. We are called to be saints: we believe in the resurrection; we accept that God has willed us to be with him for all eternity. And there are a host of those who have been through the prior ages of mankind to whom we humanly feel we can attribute the term 'holy'. These we can feel surely to be with Jesus in the glory of God the Father, expressing some of the sense of praise, joy and enthralment which is voiced in Revelation.

It is not always so easy to know about everybody else. Here we come into the realm of faith and hope. We believe in the resurrection. We believe that God died for all mankind, past, present and to come. But is this true of so-and-so who died last year, of my friend who was knocked down in the street and killed, of all those fighting in wars, of ordinary people who seem neither very good nor very bad? Are they living in the Lord, taken to highest heaven? Should we pray for them, or with them?

Throughout the whole of this month, we have a chance to think about life after death, what it takes to be a saint, our union in prayer with all those who are in the body of Christ, living and dead. We may go further than that and begin to realise that as Christ is Lord of all the world, so he has left us, his people, with the task of accepting him and his kingdom,while trying to spread it throughout the world.

While all praying covers a great variety of attitudes and responses both to God and our neighbour, in this month we can benefit considerably if

165

we concentrate upon the remarkable union that there is among us, and how this can be strengthened both through prayer and also through the loving care we can give to others in the many troubles and deprivations of living today. We are (or should be) indeed a communion or community. We are not alone. The more we pray together and pray for each other and realise in our minds and hearts the unity of the mystical body of Christ ... the more we shall help the people of the world to be one in love and service of God and each other.

All Saints

God, whom all the saints adore, assembled in thy glorious presence from all times and places of thy dominion; who gathered us far dwellers of the islands of the sea into the kingdom of thy Son; and has adorned our land with many splendid lamps of holiness; grant us worthily to celebrate the saints of our country by following their footsteps throughout the world and here, wherever thou shalt send us, each lowly serving, till all nations confess thy Name and all humankind know and fulfill its destiny in Christ; to whom with thee and the Holy Spirit be all honour and glory, world without end.

Alexander Nairne
written for the dedication of Westcott House Chapel, Cambridge (1926)

Reading: Rev 19:1-9 Song of the great crowd in heaven.

All Souls

Lord God, you have created all men, women and children. You have made us for yourself. Now, Lord, we know that many of those we love are in your care, because they have gone from this life and world to your kingdom. We so much hope and trust they are now at peace in the joy of your love. Especially, I personally want to commend to you . . . *(Put in name or names of those dead persons close to your heart)* I loved him/her/them so much, Lord. I trust for him/her/them the mercy and forgiveness of your love.

Reading: Wis 3:1-9 The souls of the virtuous are in the hands of God,
or: 1 Pet 1:3-6 A living hope through the resurrection of Jesus Christ.

A prayer for those who die young

Now and again in my life, Lord Jesus, I meet a sad, sudden and early death. You raised the son of the widow to life. This does not always happen in our experience. I want to pray now, Lord, for any who have died before their time, young in years. Especially, I want to recall to you . . . *(insert name)*. Help the family too, that they may accept the loss and still trust in you.

Reading: Wis 4:7-17 Early death, or Lk 7:11-17. The widow of Nairn.

Christ freed man from death

God called man and still calls him to an eternal imperishable communion of his whole nature with the divine life. This is the victory Christ gained in rising from the dead, since by dying himself, he freed man from death. To any thinking man, then, to offer faith supported by solid reasons is to offer an answer to his anxieties about his future destiny. At the same time it is to offer him the means of communion in Christ with his loved ones already dead, since faith gives hope that they have attained true life with God.

From the *Pastoral Constitution on the Church in the Modern World*
(Gaudium et Spes) (1965)

Reading: Rom 6:1-11 Having died with Christ, we shall return to life.

Union in prayer

I know that all who love Jesus Christ are united by his Spirit and I thank you, Lord, for this knowledge. I know that in prayer I hold those who have died, in you, in your love, and they hold me in this way too. I do not know whether humanly this is called praying with or for the dead, but I know it is the way I pray with and for those who are my friends in this life. Lord, continue to give me the great grace of experiencing this union in you with all those I love, whether alive or dead, and help me to explain to others the wonder and warmth of this way of prayer.   Amen.

Reading: Mt 18:10-20 Their angels in heaven.

The face of God

Out of the hidden depths of my soul
To you, O hidden God, I cry — hear my prayer . . .
Only show me your face, let me see your face!
. . . I would drink of the source of all sources,
I long to bathe in the light of all lights . . .
Your face, *your* face I crave to see.

Jewish Prayer

Reading: Ps 27:4-9 Lord, I seek your face.

Praying for each other

Lord God, you have commanded long ago that we love each other. I feel this relationship of love when I pray for other people. I sense you there in the middle of my prayer, because you are interested in those for whom I pray. I offer you myself in prayer for them, individual and particular, and also for every one together. Lord, hear my prayer.

Reading: Acts 10:9-23 Teach us to pray for others.

The communion of saints

O God our Lord, from whom neither life nor death can separate those who trust in thy love, and whose love holds in its embrace thy children in this world and the next; so unite us to thyself that in fellowship with thee we may always be united to our loved ones whether here or there; give us courage, constancy and hope; through him who died and was buried and rose again for us, Jesus Christ our Lord.

William Temple (1881-1944)

Reading: Jn 14:1-4 In my Father's house there are many rooms.

On judging by appearances

We should not judge the poor by their clothes and their outward appearance nor by their mental capacity, since they are often ignorant and uncouth. On the contrary, if you consider the poor in the light of faith, then you will see that they take the place of God the Son, who chose to be poor.

St. Vincent de Paul (*c.* 1580-1660)
from *Writings*

Reading: Jas 2:1-9 Poor according to the world.

Building bridges between people

Lord, whoever said 'no man is an island' was surely wrong. There are so many who are alone and lonely in a sea of people, often in towns where no one at all notices them. They can so easily become desert islands, empty and dry. Teach us how to build bridges to each other or at least to visit lonely islands in our small boats. You created us to be social creatures, and now our ways of life cut us off from each other. Show me how to relate to the isolated and stop me from ever being cut off from my fellow human beings. You made us and you care for us, and with your aid we can grow in love and concern for each other so that none remain lonely cut-off islands.

Reading: Jas 2:14-26 The merciful need have no fear.

NOVEMBER 11

Remembering the dead who died in war

Lord, why is there war? Why do we, human beings born out of the depth of your love, turn against each other and bring bloodshed and agony and despair to so many? I do not think I will ever understand how this can be, and yet I know that I am part of it. Sometimes I am sulky and ignore people; sometimes I am angry and hit out; sometimes I am contemptuous and despise people, which makes them hit back. So I am in the middle of war in myself, in my family and in all those around — and I see that we are all in it together. So my prayer today, Lord, is that somehow by the love of your Spirit you will fill my mind and heart, and the mind and heart of others with a determined will to work for peace. And today, I want to pray for all those who have died in wars past and present, just or unjust. We cannot say what they were thinking, where their heart was pleading. But, Lord, after the horror of shot and shell, give them peace in your everlasting love.

Reading: 2 Mac 12:38-45 The thought was holy and devout.
or Micah 4:1-7 No more war.

NOVEMBER 12

Belief in the resurrection of the dead

So many of those I love have died and gone from the present touch and reality of the today in which we live, Lord. There are some who cannot believe that they will ever meet again the love of their life; there are those who are just full of doubt and dismay and emptiness and loss. For all these, Lord, I pray your Spirit to bring understanding and peace. For those who are happy enough to be able to believe in life after death, I ask that you strengthen their certainty that they may speak tellingly of your eternal love. For me, Lord, I just ask you that I may trust you more.

Jesus said to Martha: 'I am the resurrection and the life' . . .

Do you believe this?

Reading: Jn 11:21-27 Life after death.

NOVEMBER 13

God is with me

God, I thank you for this time of prayer, when I become conscious of your presence, and lay before you my desires, my hopes, and my gratitude. This consciousness, this inner certainty of your presence is my greatest blessing. My life would be empty if I did not have it, if I lost you in the maze of the world, and I did not turn to you from time to time, to be at one with you, certain of your existence and your love. It is good that you are with me in all my difficulties and troubles and that I have in you a friend whose help is sure and whose love never changes.

From *Forms of Prayer for Jewish Worship*

Reading: Lam 3:21-26 It is good that one should wait quielty.

Knowing the presence of God in distress

O God, the Father everlasting, who in thy wonderous grace, standest within the shadows, keeping watch over thine own; grant that in every peril and perplexity, in our groping and weariness we may know the comfort of thy prevading presence. When the day grows dark may we in fear no evil because thy hand is upon us. Lead us onwards through the darkness into thy light, through the sorrows into the joy of the Lord, and through the cross of sacrifice into closer communion with thy Son, Jesus Christ our Lord.

John Hunter (1849-1917)
from *Devotional Services* (1892)

Reading: Jn 14:27-31 Peace I leave you.

The feast of St. Albert the Great

'Do this in remembrance of me.' There are two points to be noted here. First, we are commanded to use this sacrament. Jesus intended this by saying, 'Do this.' In the second place we do it in memory of his going to death for us.

So he said, 'Do this.' He could not have laid down a commandment more profitable or delightful, one more healthful or attractive, one more like to life eternal. We shall study these point by point.

The sacrament profits us by forgiving our sins, and is of utmost use to us by the outpouring of grace in our life. 'The Father of spirits . . . disciplines us for our good, that we may share his holiness.' Christ's holiness lies in his sacrificial action, that is, he offered himself in the sacrament: to his Father to redeem us; to us for our use. 'For their sake I consecrate myself', he said. 'Christ, who through the eternal Spirit offered himself without blemish to God, will purify our conscience from dead works to serve the living God.'

St. Albert the Great (1206-1280)
from *On St. Luke's Gospel*

Reading: Lk 22:14-20 The Last Supper.

171

The feast of St. Edmund, Archbishop and scholar

Almighty God, who didst bestow upon thy servant Edmund the perfect gifts of human and divine charity, together with the understanding of excellent mysteries; grant to us that we likewise, in the doing of thy will, may understand thy doctrine, increasing in fellowship one with another and in love towards thee, and in all sound and profitable learning.

Austin Farrer (+1968)
when he was chaplain of St. Edmund Hall, Oxford

Reading: 1 Jn 5:1-5 Love.

Keep my faith strong

You, Lord, are my hope
And in you alone do I put my trust;
You will protect me from all danger
And from every kind of trouble which can hurt my soul.
There is uncertainty all around me
And so little hope for the future,
But I know that you will be with me.
You will show me a way
Where no way seems to exist.
Keep my faith strong
And if it weakens, strengthen it;
And help me always to remember
To praise and to thank you for your care and protection.

Reading: Ps 16:1-3, 9-12 Look after me, God.

Help me to realise your presence

Teach me to live in dependence on you, trusting in you and not on my own resources. So often I forget that you are in control, both in history and in creation. You have always brought your people out of their difficulties even when things seemed hopeless. Help me to realise that you are with me every moment of the day supporting and guiding me. I thank you for your help in the past and I know that you will be always with me in the future.   Amen.

Reading: Ps 19 Wash out my hidden faults.

We take refuge in thee

From this fog-bound earth of ours
We take refuge in thee.
O rest of our souls,
Escaping like birds from a broken cage
Where thou dwellest, and with thee
Find release from meaness of spirit,
From jealousy, slander, hypocrisy,
From selfish ambition,
From the insidious darkness that broods
And breeds in our wills and hides
The vision of good and the pathway of peace.
We take refuge in thee:
Let us walk honestly in the daylight.

John S. Hoyland (1887-1957)

Reading: Ps 31 Prayer in time of ordeal.

A prayer for all creation

The story of creation opens in scripture a huge vision of powers and dominations beyond anything or anybody we can imagine. My mind ponders on the vastness of creation. Looking at the stars and listening to the exploits of astronauts, I am all the more aware of the vastness beyond my human grasp. Today, I pray to you, Lord God of all creation, that you open my mind and the minds of all men and women to the possibility of so much of wonder and joy beyond what we know now. I want to pray for all those who may exist unknown to me. I want to pray for all those who have died and gone ahead to your kingdom. I want you, Lord, to ask all those you know whom I do not — to pray for me . . . to pray for us.

Reading: Is 40:12-26 Lift your eyes and look.

Who is holy, Lord?

I have known many holy men and women in my lifetime. Not all of them seemed to believe in you, Lord Jesus, or even in your Father — God. But there was something about them of goodness. To me they were holy people. I pray for them and with them, Lord, though they do not know me. I believe there is more communion in prayer than any of us really understand. If I am right, please let this prayer develop. If I am wrong, I trust you to show me, Lord God.

Reading: Mt 22:1-14 The wedding feast.

NOVEMBER 22

The feast of St. Cecilia, patroness of music

Today we remember St. Cecilia who 'sang to you in her heart'. We praise you for the gift of music, which like poetry can lift us beyond ordinary words and thoughts towards you. We thank you for those who compose music, for those who perform it, for the faculties you have given us for appreciating it, and for the great variety of music there is so that most of us can find some to enjoy. We thank you too that music can bring us closer together and encourage us to grow in harmony with each other. Help us to use music to deepen our perception of you, to praise you in community, and to come like Saint Cecilia to live our lives with a song to you always in our hearts.

Reading: Ps 150 Praise the Lord with music.

NOVEMBER 23

Kindle us, Lord

Lord, give us, we beseech thee, in the name of Jesus Christ, thy Son our Lord, that love which can never cease, that will kindle our lamps but not extinguish them, that they may burn in us and enlighten others. Do thou, O Christ, our dearest Saviour, thyself kindle our lamps, that they may evermore shine in thy temple, that they may receive unquenchable light from thee that will enlighten our darkness and lessen the darkness of the world. Lord Jesus, we pray thee, give thy light to our lamps, that in its light the most holy place may be revealed to us in which thou dwellest as the eternal priest, that we may always behold thee, desire thee, look upon thee in love, and long after thee, for thy sake.

St. Columba (+597)

Reading: Lk 11:33-36 The parable of the lamp.

NOVEMBER 24

United with the Saints

The first wish then, which the memory of the saints inspires in us and urges us to achieve is that we should enjoy their hoped-for company, striving to deserve to be fellow-citizens with and members of the household of the spirits of the blessed . . . in a word, to be united in the communion of all the saints.

St. Bernard (1090-1153)
from a *Sermon*

Reading: 1 Cor 1:1-3 Called to take their place among all the saints.

On perfection

It is the mark of the soul that is sensitive to the love of God ever to seek the glory of God in its fulfilment of every commandment, and to delight in its own abasement, since to God, on account of his greatness, belongs glory, and to man belongs abasement whereby we become members of the household of God. If we do that, we too will rejoice, like Saint John the Baptist, in the glory of the Lord, and begin to say increasingly: 'He must increase, but I must decrease.'

Diadochus of Photike
from *On Perfection*

Reading: Jn 3:25-36 I must grow less.

The feast of St. Columba

Alone with none but thee, my God,
I journey on my way;
what need I fear if thou art near,
O King of night and day?
For safe am I within thy hand
than if a host did round me stand.

Reading: Lk 10:1-11 The missionary's instructions.

Knowing myself

Lord Jesus, eternal word of the Father,
you have brought us the good news of the heavenly Father,
and revealed him to us.
Help me, through your word,
to know you and know myself.
Let me see my wretchedness and your mercy,
my sin and your grace,
my poverty and your wealth,
my weakness and your strength,
my folly and your wisdom,
my darkness and your light.

J. Arndt (18th century)

Reading: Ps 119:8-40 Open my eyes.

The work of the Church abroad

O God, who has made of one blood
all nations of men to dwell

on the face of the earth,
and sent your blessed Son to preach peace
to them that are far off, and to them that are near;
grant that all peoples of the world
may feel after you and find you;
and hasten, O Lord, the fulfilment of your promise
to pour out your Spirit upon all flesh;
through Jesus Christ our Lord.

Adapted from
George E. L. Cotton (1813-1866)

Reading: Acts 2:14-24 Preaching the gospel of Jesus Christ.

NOVEMBER 29

The Church in our land and in the wider world

We thank you for those who brought the Christian faith to our land, and especially at this time of year, we remember the Celtic missionairies who came to Scotland and preached the gospel of your Son Jesus Christ, and whose followers kept the flame of faith alive in difficult and dark days.

We are grateful to all who bear witness to you throughout the world in a generation which is confused and discouraged; teach us how we, by our lives and example, may show forth our belief in you in our own little worlds. Give us courage and strength like the early missionaries and apostles who were not discouraged by being mocked nor by the thought of dying for you.   Amen.

Reading: 2 Cor 11:21b-32 & 12:10

NOVEMBER 30

St. Andrew, apostle and martyr

Lord Jesus, you have given the church the examples of the apostles to learn from; today when we commemorate Saint Andrew who brought to you his brother Simon Peter, and later certain Greeks as well as the boy with the barley loaves and fishes, show me how I can bring others to know and love you. Andrew, who was quieter and more in the background than his impetuous brother, can teach us how we may learn from you through humble attentiveness and through living all our lives with you by our side. Help me, Lord, to know you more deeply so that when I go to bring my friends to you I will really be able to show them what you are like. Teach me, so that I may teach others.

Reading: Jn 1:35-42 Meeting Jesus.

Index

177

Acknowledgements

George Appleton, *Jersualem Prayers for the World Today*, SPCK (1974). Reprinted by permission of The Society for Promoting Christian Knowledge.

George Appleton, *One Man's Prayers*, SPCK (1977). Reprinted by permission of The Society for Promoting Christian Knowledge.

George Appleton, *The Word is the Seed*, SPCK (1976). Reprinted by permission of The Society for Promoting Christian Knowledge.

William Barclay, *Prayers for the Christian Year*, SCM Press (1974). Reprinted by permission of SCM Press Ltd.

Karl Barth, *Deliverence to the Captives*, SCM Press (1961). Reprinted by permission of SCM Press Ltd.

Anthony Bloom, *Living Prayer*, published and © Darton, Longman & Todd Limited, and is ured by permission of the publishers.

Rex Chapman, *A Kind of Praying*, SCM Press (1970). Reprinted by permission of SCM Press Ltd.

Frank Colquhoun (ed.) *Contemporary Parish Prayers*, Hodder & Stoughton (1975). Reprinted by permission of Hodder & Stoughton Limited.

Kenneth Grahame, *Wind in the Willows*, (Ch. 7), Methuen Children's Books Ltd. (1971), © text copyright University Chest, Oxford. Reprinted by permission of Associated Book Publishers Ltd.

Nicholas Grou, *How to Pray*, James Clarke & Co. Reprinted by permission of James Clarke & Co. Ltd.

Dag Hammarskjöld, *Markings*, (translated by W. H. Auden and Leif Sjöberg). Reprinted by permission of Faber and Faber Ltd.

Perry D. Le Fevre (ed.), *The Prayers of Kierkegaard*, The University of Chicago Press (1956). Reprinted by permission of The University of Chicago Press.

Alistair Maclean, *Hebridean Altars*, W & R Chambers. Reprinted by permission of W. & R. Chambers Ltd.

John Mbiti, *Prayers of African Religion*, SPCK (1975). Reprinted by permission of The Society for Promoting Christian Knowledge.

Caryl Micklem (ed.), *Contemporary Prayers for Public Worship*, SCM Press (1967). Reprinted by permission of SCM Press Ltd.

181